THE MAKING OF LATIN

THE MAKING OF LATIN

AN INTRODUCTION TO LATIN, GREEK AND ENGLISH ETYMOLOGY

BY R. S. CONWAY, F.B.A.

LITT.D.(CANTAB.), HON. LITT.D.(DUB.)

HULME PROFESSOR OF LATIN AND INDO-EUROPEAN PHILOLOGY IN
THE UNIVERSITY OF MANCHESTER, HON. FELLOW OF
GONVILLE AND CAIUS COLLEGE, CAMBRIDGE

College Classical Series

ARISTIDE D. CARATZAS, PUBLISHER

NEW ROCHELLE, NEW YORK

1983

A reprint of the 1923 edition
published by John Murray, London

This edition published by
Aristide D. Caratzas, Publisher
Caratzas Publishing Co., Inc.
481 Main Street (P.O. Box 210)
New Rochelle, New York 10802

ISBN: 0-89241-341-7 (paper); 0-89241-335-2 (cloth)

PREFACE

THE object of this little book is to explain as simply as possible the principles of the modern Science of Language, and to indicate the chief results of these principles in the study of Latin, with some of the consequences in that of English and the Romance languages.

This new knowledge has been current for some forty years, but it has been treated hitherto as a privilege suited only for students doing highly specialised work. For this restriction I can see no reason beyond the well-known unwillingness of the specialist to explain his subject to non-specialist readers. The truth is that few things add more interest even to the elements of a language than the good salt of a little etymology. But since it has become generally known that the derivations given in the current dictionaries and in many commentaries are based on pious theories framed long before the advent of scientific method, the best teachers are apt to be shy of etymology altogether.

This book is meant to be easily understood by anyone who has learnt enough to find his way about Latin authors with the help of a dictionary. The Greek examples given are everywhere translated, and are such, I venture to hope, as will be interesting even to beginners in Greek. The size, plan and method of the chapters and sections have been influenced by practical experience of teaching the subject to a variety of classes and pupils in Cambridge, Cardiff and Manchester. In choosing both matter and examples I have tried to keep before me the point of view

of an intelligent set of boys and girls of about fifteen, as
well as the needs of older students; so that the book
might serve as the basis of a short series of lessons—
between thirty and forty should suffice—in any Classical
VI Form or in any class doing Latin work above what has
come to be known as 'Matriculation-standard.'

English-speaking students especially have much to gain
from the study of Latin Etymology. Their own language
is so largely based on Latin that their understanding of it
is deepened and enlivened by knowing the history of Latin
words and idioms; and all the time they are increasing
their enjoyment, and consequently their profit, in reading
Latin authors. To know, for instance, that English *quick*
is close akin to Latin *vivus* (§ 1) and once meant 'living';
that *temere* (§ 2) (whence English *temerity*) means 'in the
dark'; that *purgāre* (from **pur-igāre* § 89) means properly
'to treat with fire,' adds a picturesque element of interest
to a multitude of passages[1] in both English and Latin writers.
One of the schoolboy's first troubles in Vergil (*Aeneid* I. 8)
may be made into a pleasure if it is explained to him
that *nūmen* is a 'portmanteau-word' (p. 113 footn.) in
which a simple derivative of *nuere* 'to nod,' meaning 'a
nod, assent, decision with authority,' has been packed into
one with the Latin equivalent of the Greek πνεῦμα 'spirit';
so that *nūmen* means, in this passage and often, neither
'decision' nor 'deity' but a fusion of the two, 'divine
will, divine intention.'

But besides the help which etymology thus gives to
interpreting Latin authors, there are many interesting
questions which a student meets directly he begins to compare English with Latin, or indeed with any Romance
language, but to which the answers have been only recently

---

[1] Of derivations which have a literary value other examples are
suādēre (§ 149); *iūmentum* (§ 191); *ratis* (§ 216); *polus* from Gr.
πόλος (§ 172); Eng. *kirk* (§ 12), *thorpe* (§ 60. 4). Examples of
special historical interest are forms like *Clōdius* (§ 114), *Sulla*
(§ 218); and I may add here the title *Augustus*, which means
literally 'huge, of superhuman stature, worshipful,' being akin
to Lat. *augēre*, Gr. αὔξειν 'to increase,' Sansk. *ōjas* 'divine
bigness, majesty.'

found, such as the nature of what is called ' Gender '
(§§ 205–11), or of the Impersonal Passive (§§ 311–2).
And many well-known stumbling-blocks in Latin usage
become natural and interesting as soon as their history is
understood ; for example the poetical use of the Distributive
Numerals (*centēnus* and the like, § 238) ; the earlier uses
of the Gerundive (§§ 237–9) ; or the frequently Present
meaning of the Participle in *-tus* (§ 233) ; or its Middle use [1]
with an Accusative (p. 127).

It is not to be expected or desired that such a book
should contain much that can be called original. My debt
on every page to my revered teacher Karl Brugmann,
especially to his *Grundriss der Vergleichenden Grammatik*
(Ed. 1, 1886–1892 ; Ed. 2, 1897–1916), and to his delight-
ful shorter treatise (*Kurze Vergleichende Grammatik* 1903–4),
and also, in Chapter VII, to Roby's great *Latin Grammar*,
will be plain to all specialists. But my endeavour has
been everywhere to express clearly the results of my
own study, indicating the evidence for each conclusion, and
distinguishing points which are only probable from those
which I count certain. For any discussion of unsettled
questions the student must look elsewhere, especially to the
books just mentioned. One of the difficulties which seem
serious in beginning the subject but trivial afterwards is
that to denote clearly the different sounds with whose
history we are concerned, a certain number of new symbols
have to be added to the Latin alphabet. Those used in
this book are explained in the course of Chapters II and
III. But it is well to state here that after careful con-
sideration I have used the signs *q* ('ku') and *g* ('gu') to
denote the 'Labialising Velars,' without the rather laborious
addition of ͧ which the more advanced student will find
necessary when he comes to discuss the relation of these
sounds to the ' Pure Velars.' In this matter the doctrine

---

[1] An interesting collection of examples of this use by Dr. Clara
M Knight will be found in *Am. Journ. Philol.*, xxxix. (1918), p. 184.
The history of the Participle was first clearly set forth by Brugmann
in a monumental article in *Indog. Forschungen* V. (1895), p. 87.

to which I incline (§ 173) is simpler, if more agnostic, than the point of view from which Brugmann has surveyed the evidence; his classification is invaluable for purposes of enquiry, but it was not meant to be final.

For the schoolboy's sake also I have retained the modern (XVI century) symbol *v* to denote the sound of consonantal *u* (Eng. *w*) in Latin.

I am deeply indebted to the kindness of my colleague Mr. G. E. K. Braunholtz whose searching and patient criticism has removed a number of obscurities and one or two serious errors. For such as may remain I am of course alone responsible. The Indices, which I hope will add to the usefulness of the book, are mainly the work of Mr. G. S. Conway, B.A., of Rugby.

I shall be grateful for any criticism from readers of the book, sent to me directly, or through its publisher, especially from those who may have used it with a class.

R. S. C.

MANCHESTER,
    August, 1922.

CONTENTS

THE
MAKING OF LATIN

I. THE KEY OF THE RIDDLE

§ **1.** ETYMOLOGY means literally 'telling the truth';
the name was invented by the Greeks to describe
the study of what they called the 'true,' that is the
original, meaning of words. For words are continually
changing their meaning; and the form, that is the
sound, of words is often changed too. For example,
the English word *quick* now means 'active, speedy';
but in Queen Elizabeth's time it meant 'living,' as
in the Biblical phrase *the quick and the dead;* and in
far earlier times, as we shall see, its form was something
like *gwīgwos* (§ **60** (4)). Now people once used to
suppose that such changes came quite by haphazard;
but we know now that in each language at any given
time the different sounds were being changed in certain
definite ways, and in no others. By finding out these
ways of change we can often discover the earlier form of
a word, and its earlier meaning also; and when we have
done this, we say we have found its D e r i v a t i o n.

§ **2.** School-boys and others often wonder what
means there are of finding out the derivations of words.

1

They can only be found when beside the word which we wish to explain there exists some other word or words either in the same language or in another kindred language, with which the word can be c o m p a r e d. By comparing two or more kindred words we can generally find out something about the earlier form of each of them. When we compare Lat. *gero, haurio* with their participles *gestus, haustus* (and when we have learnt that in Latin -*s*- between vowels became -*r*-), we see that their earlier forms were **geso, *hausio ;* so if we set *temere* ' rashly ' beside Sanskrit *tamas* ' darkness,' when we have learnt that *a* in Sanskrit regularly corresponds to any one of the three vowels, *a, e,* or *o*, in Latin, we see that *temere* meant originally ' in the dark.'

§ **3.** By Kindred Languages we mean those which have descended from a common ancestor. Thus what are called Romance languages, Corsican, Sardinian, Spanish, Portuguese, French, Italian and Roumanian, are kindred languages because they have all descended from Latin. But they did not all begin their separate growth at the same date. The oldest are Corsican and Sardinian, which took their rise from the Latin of the Roman camps which were established in those islands between the First and Second Punic Wars in 231 B.C. Then comes Spanish : for Spain became a Roman Province at the end of the Second Punic

---

* Observe this convenient use of the asterisk. We attach * to forms which are not actually on record but whose former existence we can infer from other forms which do appear in literature or inscriptions.

War, in 197 B.C. Then France, of which the oldest dialect (Provençal) dates from the establishment of the *provincia Narbonensis* in 121 B.C. Latest of all began Roumanian which was started by the conquest of Dacia by the Emperor Trajan : this was completed in 107 A.D. and was commemorated by the great Column of Trajan which is still standing in Rome.

The relation between Latin and all these languages is sometimes expressed by using the word *proethnic* which means ' before the separation of the nations ' ; Latin is ' pro-ethnic Romance.'

§ **4.** In just the same way nearly all the languages of Europe, and some of the languages of India and Persia, have descended from a language which we call Indo-European. But unluckily we have no direct record of this language : we can only infer what it was by comparing the different branches of language which sprang from it, Indo-Persian, Armenian, Greek, Italic, Keltic, Germanic and Balto-Slavonic (p. 127).

§ **5.** The oldest branch of Indo-Persian is Sanskrit, the sacred language of the Brahmins of India ; and their most sacred document is the Rig-Veda or ' Book of Hymns,' the oldest parts of which are judged to be as old as 1500 B.C.

§ **6.** By Greek we generally mean Attic, the language of ancient Athens : but the other dialects, Ionic, Doric, and Aeolic, often had more primitive forms. Attic spread over all the coasts of the Mediterranean, and by the conquests of Alexander the Great, who died in 323 B.C., over the whole of Asia Minor and even further East. This wide-spread language was called the *Koinē*, that is ' the common dialect ' ; and from this is descended Modern Greek.

§ 7. Keltic includes in one branch Gallic, an ancient language of Gaul, of which we have only scanty records, and also Welsh and Breton : this branch is called ' Brythonic.' In the other branch, which is called ' Goidelic,' are Manx, Irish, and the Gaelic of the Scotch Highlands. Breton, Welsh, Irish and Gaelic are still spoken languages.

§ 8. The earliest Germanic tongue known to us is Gothic, recorded in the translation of the New Testament made by Bishop Ulfila, a missionary to the Goths of the Crimea in the 4th century A.D. ; other branches are Icelandic, Norwegian, Danish, English (of which ' Scotch ' is a dialect), Dutch, and German.

§ 9. Latin is the best known language of the Italic Branch, in which are included besides Latin several dialects, called Oscan, Umbrian, Volscian, Sabine and Faliscan, which are known to us from inscriptions and from scattered statements of grammarians. It is often possible to discover the original form and meaning of a Latin word by comparing it with the kindred word in one of these dialects. For instance, North Osc. *prismu* ' first ' shows that Lat. *prīmus* has lost an -*s*- before its -*m*- (§ 193) and contains the stem *pris*- that we see in *pris-cus* ' primitive ' (§ 252).

Changes in Language

§ 10. From the examples already given it will be clear that by comparing kindred languages we often discover changes of sound that have taken place in the growth of each. These changes are of two kinds which it is very important to distinguish.

The first kind of change happens unconsciously without the speakers of the language knowing that any change has happened at all. Thus Lat. *rēgem* became in French *roi :* and we find that the same change happened to Lat. *ē* in all words in which it stood in an accented syllable. The statement of any such change (in this case that " Lat. *ē* when accented became *oi* in French ") is called a Phonetic Law. The loss of the -*g*- and of the -*em* of *rēgem* happened also through phonetic changes, or, as we say, ' by Phonetic Laws.'

§ **11.** Strictly speaking Phonetic Laws have no exceptions : that is to say, a phonetic change affects equally the same sound in all words existing in the language at the time, provided that the sound is under the same conditions in all the words. Thus Lat. -*ē*- became Fr. -*oi*- when the *e* was accented, as it was in Lat. *rḗgem* (see § **85** (2)), but not otherwise. Thus Lat. *mē, tē, sē,* became Fr. *moi, toi, soi,* when they were emphatic and therefore accented, but Fr. *me, te, se,* when they were unaccented.

§ **12.** But it often happens that words containing the sound affected by a particular phonetic change are introduced into a language (sometimes from being borrowed from another language) after the phonetic change has ceased or, as it is often stated, ' after the Phonetic Law has expired.'

For example, the word *kirk* was introduced (or

re-introduced) into English from Scotch many centuries after the change of *k* to *ch* in English, which produced the English word *church* from the same original word, which in Latin was *cyriaca* (Gr. κυριακή ' the house of the Lord '), Anglo-Saxon *cirice*.

§ **13.** In that case in modern English we have what is called a D o u b l e t—two words of different form, derived from the same original and existing side by side, often with a slight difference of meaning which gives the key to their history. And it is generally the borrowed word, in this case *kirk*, which has the narrower and more precise meaning. Now in Latin a great many words were borrowed from the neighbouring dialects, especially Oscan and Sabine, and many from Greek : and many of them have a shape which is different from what they would have had if they had existed in Latin all along. For example, *rūfus* ' red-haired ' is a borrowed word (§ **177**) and shows a narrower meaning than the pure Latin *ruber* ' red ' which is closely related to it. We saw in § **11** another type of Doublet (Fr. *moi* and *me*) due to different conditions of Accent.

§ **14.** But there is another kind of change which is, generally at least, partly conscious, that is to say, present to the minds of many speakers when the change is made. This is due to the influence of Analogy, which is the great constructive and reconstructive force in human speech. How it operates can best be shown by a few examples. We know from kindred words that the Latin numeral corresponding to Eng. *nine* was to start with **noven* (hence *nōnus* ' ninth ' from *novenos*) ; but it was changed to *novem* so as to match *septem* and *decem* in which -*m* was original (cf. Lat. *septimus, decimus :* Sansk. *saptamas,* ' seventh ' ; *daçamas,* ' tenth ').

§ **15.** Very often these Analogical changes modify the results of a Phonetic Law and so produce apparent exceptions to it. In Latin in words of two syllables (' Disyllables ') whose first syllable was short like *via* and *modus,* the second syllable of the Ablative was shortened by a phonetic change (§§ **95, 96**). But in words like *dominus* and *mensa* which had more than two syllables, or a long first syllable, this phonetic change did not take place, so that the abl. remained *mensā, dominō :* and these words were far more numerous than the words of the shape of *via, modus.*

Hence people felt that in the First and Second Declensions the meaning of the abl. required -*ā* or -*ō* to express it properly : and so they would not allow themselves or their children to pronounce anything but a long vowel in the Abl., even of words like *via* or *modus.* We state this process shortly by saying that the -*ā* in *viā* and the -*ō* in *modō* were " restored by Analogy."

§ **16.** But meanwhile the word *modo* had come to be used not only as an ablative meaning ' by ' (or ' on ') ' the proper line ' but as an adverb meaning ' just, only ' : and in this meaning it was no longer felt by the general body of speakers, or as we say ' in the popular consciousness,' to be an ablative. Hence in the adverb the short -*o* produced by phonetic change was left unaltered. Exactly the same phonetic

B

change affected the nominative and accusative neut.
plur. of disyllabic words, such as *bŏna, ĕa*, in which we
know from kindred languages that the *-a* was originally
long.

§ 17. But in the compound word *intereā* ' among
those things, meanwhile,' which had become an adverb,
the original long *-a* remained. It was not affected
by the phonetic change, because the word had four
syllables ; and as it had come to be felt merely as an
adverb, no longer as a preposition and a pronoun,
it was not affected by the analogical change which
spread the short *-a* of the very common disyllabic
words *ĕă, bŏnă, mălă, mĕă, tŭă, sŭă* through all the
neuter plurals of pronouns (like *illa*), nouns (like
dōna), and adjectives (like *multa*). Words like *intereā*
and *modo* which became separated in consciousness
from the sets of forms (in a Declension or Conjugation)
to which they once belonged are said to have been
"i s o l a t e d" or "c r y s t a l l i s e d." They are
often a great help to our study, because in these we have
true phonetic forms preserved of which otherwise we
might know nothing.

§ 18. The examples just given show the power of
Analogy both to restore and to innovate. In Ablatives
like *viā* the old quantity was put back on the pattern
of words like *mensā* (§ 15) ; but in all the Neut. Plurals
of the Second Declension the final *-a*, originally long,
has been shortened to match that of the disyllables
like *ĕă* (§ 17).

§ 19. Such modification by Analogy of what we
may call the natural form which words have taken

by unconscious Phonetic change is particularly common in Compound words. By a phonetic change (§ **122**) the final *-o-* of the first half of compounds like *agro-cola ' tiller of the fields ' became *-i-* so that we know the word only as *agri-cola*.

Thus a type was established for the great mass of compounds, so that we get words like *foedi-fragus*, ' treaty-breaking ' from *foedus, foederis* ' treaty,' where logically the first part ought to have been *foeder-*. Just in the same way in Greek in the very numerous compounds like μῡθολόγος, ' a teller of ancient stories ' and μῡθολογίᾱ ' the knowledge of stories, mythology,' or ἀστρολογίᾱ ' the knowledge of the stars,' hence 'astrology,' the final *-o-* of the first part of the word came to be felt as part of the ending ; hence new words were made like φυσιολογίᾱ ' physiology ' from φύσις ' native power, nature,' instead of *φυσιλογίᾱ, which would have been correct. Hence in English came the names for the different sciences which are sometimes called the " -ologies."

§ **20.** So it is common in compound verbs to have the form of the simple verb restored. For example in Latin *dēlēnio* is restored on the pattern of the simple *lēnio*, instead of *dēlĭnio* which would have been the true phonetic form (§ **129**). Such restored forms are called Re-formates.

§ **21.** Again by a regular phonetic change (§ **134**) *claudo* became in compounds *clūdo* (*conclūdo, exclūdo, inclūdo, reclūdo*) ; but these words were so much commoner than the simple *claudo* that before the time of Juvenal the form *claudo* had died out altogether, and been replaced by *clūdo*, which was taken from the compounds. So *plicāre* instead of **plecere* (Gr. πλέκω) or of **plocāre*, from *explicāre, complicāre*. This process is sometimes called D e c o m p o s i t i o n.

§ 22. The same kind of reasoning by Analogy often conceals the true history of a word. From the negative adjectival compounds *in-decēns*, ' unbecoming,' *improbus* ' not excellent, bad,' were created the verbs *indecet* ' it mis-becomes, is unfitted,' *improbo* ' I count bad, I disapprove,' which came to be felt as compounds of *decet* and *probo*. From the adjective *operātus* ' full of work, seriously occupied,' which was derived from *opera* ' work ' as *ansātus* ' handled ' from *ansa* ' handle,' but which looked very much like a participle (such as *hortātus, pālātus*) there was formed later on the Deponent verb *operāri* ' to devote oneself to (some duty).' Such new words are called R e t r o f o r - m a t e s.

§ 23. It is to be noted carefully that all the changes which have been described are changes of Sound, taking place in the spoken language, often long before the epoch in which the language was written down. When a language comes to be written down, and fixed spelling is established,—a thing which has happened to the languages of all civilised peoples,—and still more when the language comes to be printed, we generally find that the sounds actually existing in speech are only roughly represented in writing or printing. This is particularly true of English. The spelling of Latin was much more exact ; but in all languages which have come to be written, when a spelling is once established, it tends to remain although the actual sound of the word may have changed. For example, the Latin word which about 200 B.C. was pronounced and written *deicō* (with its first syllable like Eng. *day*) was frequently still so written in the time of Cicero, when it had long been pronounced *dīcō* (with its first syllable like Eng. *Dee*). For this and other reasons the history of the alphabet or alphabets used to write a language is something quite different from, although sometimes connected with, the history of the language.

NOTE i

For example, the sign which in the Latin and English alphabet represents the sound *f*, namely F, had once, in all the various Greek alphabets, represented a different sound, that of Eng. *w*. If we ask how the sign came to change its value, we find that the Etruscans, when in the 7th or 8th Century B.C. they took a Greek alphabet to write their own language which possessed a sound very much like Lat. *f*, found no sign in the Greek alphabet for that sound. The best they could do was to combine two of the Greek signs F and ☐ (the older form of H) which together properly denoted the sound of Eng. *wh* (pronounced fully and truly as it still is by the educated class in Edinburgh). This make-shift way of writing the sound *f* appears not merely in Etruscan inscriptions, but in the oldest of all the Latin inscriptions we possess, on the golden brooch found in 1871 in a tomb at Praeneste which archaeologists ascribe to about 600 B.C. The inscription runs thus :

manios med fhe-fhaked numasioi

This would be in classical Latin ' Manius me fecit Numerio ' (on the Dative form see § 118 NOTE ; on the Perfect §§ 297 and 71). But the Romans, as by degrees they came to decide on an alphabet for Latin, with the help of their neighbours (who at that epoch

were also their rulers), the Etruscans and of their somewhat
more distant neighbours the Greeks of Cumæ in Campania, did
not use Ϝ, as the Greeks and Etruscans did, to mean *w*; so they
saw no reason for the cumbrous Ϝꓯ, and wrote simply Ϝ to
mean *f*.

All this story of the sign Ϝ is important for the study of the
beginnings of civilisation at Rome. But it tells us very little,
if anything, that we did not know about Latin as a language ;
though of course, if we had not known what the sound of Ϝ
in Latin was, we should welcome the evidence of the spelling
wh as showing that it was a sound 'with an h in it,' i.e. (§§ 25, 52)
that it was Breathed. And for the study of Etruscan, of which
we still know only a little, the evidence is important.

This example will serve to show that the history of the signs
of the alphabet in which a language is written is something
quite distinct from the history of the language ; and it is the
history of the language which governs Etymology, and with
which this book is concerned.

Note ii

The body of principles which have been briefly explained
here (§§ 10–23) is the work of what used to be called the ' new
school ' of Philologists of whom Karl Brugmann of Leipzig who
died in 1919 was the greatest. They made Philology an exact
science, because their discovery of the invariability of Phonetic
Law made it for the first time possible to apply strict tests to
any proposed derivation. We ask now, does the suggested
derivation accord with the known Phonetic Laws of the language
concerned ? Or, if it seems to make an exception to any one of
them, can the reason for such an exception be found, for instance,
in the influence of Analogy ? Or, if it involves our recognising
a new Phonetic Law, are there any forms which would contradict
the new Law and for which no explanation can be found ? For
example, it was once supposed that the forms of the Latin Passive
contained the word *sē*; *amor* 'I am loved ' was derived from
" *amō sē*." Not to mention a host of other obvious objections

we should have to assume that the final -ē of the supposed "amōsē" was lost after the -s- had become -r-. But there are a multitude of forms of precisely the same shape in Latin, i.e. forms which end with two long syllables, the last being a long vowel (e.g. amantī, sevērē) which show that a long vowel was preserved, not lost, in such a position. Hence we can say quite certainly that for this reason, even if there were no other, the supposed derivation cannot be the true one. (On the real origin of the Passive see § 311.)

The first result of the recognition of the strictness of Phonetic Laws was to destroy a great number of derivations which had been long taught and of which many still linger in the dictionaries. But the greater knowledge which scientific methods of study have produced, has given us a far larger number of trustworthy derivations than those which it obliged us to discard.

Even the brief summary of the Phonetic Laws of Latin which this Introduction gives will enable us to apply serious tests to any proposed derivation of a Latin word and, generally, to say whether the changes of sound which it would lead us to assume did or did not take place in Latin at the date suggested. And we shall further realise the kind of questions that must be asked and answered before we can be sure of the truth of a proposed derivation in any language. So far as Greek and English are concerned, we shall have to notice a number of their most important Phonetic Laws in the course of our study of Latin.

II. WHAT IS SPEECH?

§ **24.** To follow the history of the sounds in any language we must understand how sounds are produced.

Just as in a whistle or an organ sound is made by a current of air passing through certain openings, and being set in vibration by certain tongues or edges put in the way of the current, so sound is produced in the human throat and mouth by a current of air sent out from the lungs ; and different kinds of sound arise from the different ways in which the current is treated as it passes through the throat and mouth.

Breath and Voice

§ **25.** In the larynx (that is, the upper end of the wind-pipe) through which the current passes, there are two wonderful pieces of soft muscle, which can be either left loose, in which case they fold themselves up against the wall of the larynx on either side, and do not affect the current of air at all ; or stretched tightly, so that the current has to pass between two crisp, straight, and almost parallel edges (but not quite parallel since they meet at one end). These are

called the Vocal Chords, or, better, the Vocal Edges.
When the Edges are relaxed and folded up the
current of air passes unmodified and inaudible into
the mouth; the current is then called B r e a t h,
and any sounds made with it in the mouth are said
to be B r e a t h e d, such as *p, t, f;* or *s* in Eng. *so,
mist* (often written *c* as in *rice*).

§ **26.** But when the current of air has to pass
between the Vocal Edges fully stretched, they vibrate
and impart their vibration to the current. This so
receives from them a musical quality, and is called
V o i c e, and the sounds which it produces are said
to be V o i c e d, such as *b, d, v;* or *z* in Eng. *size*
(often written *s*, as in *is, rose*).

§ **27.** The Vocal Edges can be stretched to different
degrees of tightness; and in singing, the higher the
note required the greater the tension; that is, the more
tightly are the Edges stretched.

Vowels, Sonants, and Consonants

§ **28.** V o w e l s are produced by V o i c e, as their
name implies, passing through the mouth while the
tongue and the lips are held in some particular p o s i-
t i o n.

For *a* (as in Eng. *father*) the tongue is low in the
mouth, its highest point being near the back. For
e (as in Eng. *men* or as in Fr. *passé*) the tongue is raised
so that its highest point is about in the middle of the
mouth. For *i* (short in Eng. *pit*, long in Eng. *machine*)
the tongue is raised high near the front of the palate.
o (as in Eng. *bond*) and *u* (as in Eng. *pull, push*) are made

very much like *a* and *e* except that the l i p s are
r o u n d e d as the Voice passes through. This is of
course only a very rough description. In nearly all
languages there are a great many intermediate positions
giving rise to special kinds of vowels.

§ **29.** When the tongue is at rest and the lips are
not moved during the passage of Voice through the
mouth, the result is a colourless or " neutral " vowel,
very common in unaccented syllables in English,
e.g. in the second syllable of such words as *suitable,
different, memory*. This vowel is conveniently denoted
by *ə*, a symbol called ' schwa,' from the name of the
sound in Hebrew.

§ **30.** The vowels are the simplest kind of
S o n a n t s. By a Sonant we mean a sound which
can by itself be pronounced as a syllable. By a
C o n s o n a n t we mean a sound which cannot be
heard unless it is combined with a Sonant. Thus the
sound *p* cannot be heard unless it is combined with
a Sonant, as in *pa*, or in *ep*.

§ **31.** All sounds except the vowels are produced
by a m o v e m e n t of the organs of the mouth (lips,
tongue, uvula), acting on a stream of either Breath
or Voice. The movement interferes with the current
in different ways.

Consonantal i and u (i̭, u̯)

§ **32.** The simplest of all Consonants are those made
by putting the tongue and lips into the position
required for the vowel *i*, or the vowel *u*, and then
abandoning the position at once while the current

of air passes, and producing another sound. Thus
we get what are called Consonant i and Consonant u,
conveniently written $i̯$ and $u̯$, always in combination with a vowel. These sounds differ very little
from those represented by the English letters y and
w (§ **45**). For instance the English word *way* begins
with $u̯$ and ends with $i̯$, and would be strictly spelt
$u̯ei̯$. Eng. *yes* begins with consonant $i̯$ and Eng. *low*
ends with consonant $u̯$. The sounds might be strictly
classed as a weak kind of Fricative (§ **35**). Hence
i and u are sometimes called Semi-Vowels to suggest
their use both as Sonants and as Consonants.

§ **33.** Where the current of air is only modified by
receiving a vibration from the tongue we get the Liquids,
r when the tip of the tongue is vibrated, and l when the
sides of the tongue are vibrated ; to produce l the front
of the tongue is generally set fast against the teeth or
palate. Eng. and Lat. r and l are both made with
Voice. In modern English the Vibration of r has
become very weak, and at the end of a syllable it is
hardly heard at all unless a vowel follows.

§ **34.** This vibration may be short and followed
immediately by a vowel ; in this case we have Consonant r and Consonant l. But the vibration may be
prolonged so as to make a syllable ; in this case we
have Sonant r and Sonant l, conveniently written $r̥$
and $l̥$. These sounds are very common in English,
though they are spelt in many ways. The last
sound of the words *collar, brother, Cheshire, motor* is
(or, at least was) a Sonant r, though in Southern
English it has sunk to little more than the neutral

vowel *ə* (§ **29**) ; and the last sound of *dual, mussel, bottle, carol* is a sonant *l*.

FRICATIVES, PLOSIVES, AND ASPIRATES

§ **35.** When a current is modified not by a musical vibration, but roughly so that it is either rubbed in passing through a narrow passage, or for a moment altogether stopped and then released, we get the two classes of sounds called Fricatives, or rubbed sounds, and Plosives, sounds with a kind of burst or explosion. For Aspirates see § **50.**

The interruption can be made at any part of the mouth by the lips or by the tongue, either alone or in combination with the teeth. We get therefore different kinds of Fricatives or Plosives according as the sound is formed by Breath or Voice, and according to the place at which the Breath or Voice is rubbed (in Fricatives) or stopped (in Plosives).

Velars, Palatals, Dentals, Interdentals, Labials

§ **36.** V e l a r consonants are formed by the tongue and the Velum, that is the soft part of the palate at the back ; e.g. the Velar Plosives Eng. *c* in *cotton* or *g* in *got*. These sounds are often followed by a conso-nant *u*, as in Eng. *quantity, anguish ;* Lat. *quod* ' what,' *unguo* ' I anoint.' Strictly they are written *q* and *g* (' gu ').

§ **37.** P a l a t a l Plosives are made when the cur-rent of the Breath or Voice is stopped by the tongue pressed against some part of the hard palate, as Eng. *k* in *kin* or *g* in *get*. Strictly they are written *k̂* and *ĝ*.

§ **38.** For P a l a t a l F r i c a t i v e s the current is not completely stopped but rubbed between the tongue and some part of the palate. The commonest kind is that of Eng. *sh* in *shut,* which is Breathed and which corresponds to the Voiced sound of Fr. *j* as in *jour,* or of Eng. *z* in *azure.* Sansk. *ç* (Breathed) and *j* (Voiced) are similar sounds. The final consonants of such German words as *ich* ‘ I,’ *weg* ‘ way ’ are Palatal Fricatives of a slightly different kind. There were no such sounds in Latin in the time of Cicero.

§ **39.** D e n t a l Plosives are made when the current of air is stopped by pressing the tongue against the back of the upper teeth, *t* Breathed and *d* Voiced.

§ **40.** But if the tongue is only brought near enough to the teeth to rub the current without completely stopping it, we get the Dental Fricatives, *s* (Breathed) as in Eng. *us, nurse* (often written *c* as in Eng. *ace*) ; *z* (Voiced) as in Eng. *size* (often written *s* as in Eng. *is, rise*).

§ **41.** If the tongue is put below the upper teeth so that the current hisses out between the interstices of the teeth, and between the teeth and the tongue, we get what are called the I n t e r d e n t a l Fricatives. In English these are represented, unfortunately, both by the same letters, *th* in *thin* (Breathed) and *th* in *then* (Voiced). These are properly written þ and ð respectively.

§ **42.** The English sounds which are roughly classed as Dentals *t, d, s, z* are not true Dentals because the tongue is brought to touch or approach not the teeth themselves but the ridge of the palate behind the teeth and strictly these English sounds are called Alveolar.

But the French *t*, *d*, *s*, *z* are true Dentals, and the
Latin *t*, *s*, *d*, *z* may have been the same.

Labio-Dentals

§ **43.** When the lower lip is pressed against the
upper teeth, and the current of air forces its way out
between them, we get the L a b i o - D e n t a l
F r i c a t i v e s, Breathed as *f* in Eng. *firm*, Lat.
firmus ; Voiced as Eng. *v* in *van*.

But note that this latter sound did not arise in Latin
from Consonant *u* until the 2nd Century A.D. (see § **153**).
In Latin at the time of Cicero Consonant *u* (which in
modern times has in Latin texts been commonly
printed *v*) was pronounced very nearly as English *w*,
that is to say, it was not Labio-Dental but a pure
Labial (§ **45**).

Labials

§ **44.** L a b i a l Plosives are made when the current
is stopped by closing the lips, *p* (Breathed), *b*
(Voiced).

§ **45.** P u r e   L a b i a l Fricatives are made by
rubbing the current between the lips, Eng. *wh* in *what*
(Breathed), *w* in *wet* (Voiced) ; note however that in
vulgar southern English *wh* is sounded as *w*.   The only
difference between this Voiced Labial Fricative (Eng. *w*)
and consonant *u* (Lat. *v* as in *venio*) is that in the Fricative the lips are held a little longer and more tightly
so that the rubbing is more severe.

NASALS

§ **46.** N a s a l sounds are produced when a portion of the current of air is allowed to escape through the nose.   The entrance to the nasal passage is above the throat at the back of the mouth ; this entrance is closed when the uvula is pressed against the back wall of the throat.   When the uvula hangs loose, part of the current escapes through the nose, or the whole current, if the mouth is closed.

§ **47.** If this passage is left open while vowels are being formed, they are given what is called a ' nasal colour ' ; this is often heard in some English dialects, especially in America and Canada.

§ **48.** When part of the Voice escapes through the nose during the formation of Voiced Plosives, we get the corresponding Nasals.   For instance *m* is the same sound as *b* except that part of the Voice escapes through the nose while the contact for *b* is being made by the lips.   *m* is therefore called ' the Voiced Labial Nasal.' *n* is the Voiced Dental Nasal, and there are also nasal sounds corresponding to the Palatal and Velar Plosives. Both of these latter nasal sounds are commonly denoted in English and in Latin merely by the letter *n* as in Lat. *ingero, unguo*, Eng. *linger, anguish.*

§ **49.** If the humming sound produced by the part of the Voice that escapes through the nose is prolonged enough to make a syllable while the part of the current that is in the mouth is still stopped we get the ' Nasal Sonants ' ; for instance *ṃ, ṇ*, which are common in English though they are spelt in many ways.   Sonant *n* occurs in the last syllable of words like *London, open,* and before a consonant in *isn't.* Sonant *m* is heard in the second syllable of *Chatham, anthem, bottom,* and is spelt by *m* alone in some words recently taken from Greek (directly or through French) like *chasm, rhythm.*

THE ASPIRATES

§ **50.** By an Aspirate we mean the combination of a Plosive with a slight emission of Breath before the next sound. This combination is conveniently represented by adding the symbol *h* to the symbols of the Plosives, *qh, gh, k̂h, ĝh, th, dh, ph, bh.* All these sounds (except the Velar *qh* and *gh*) exist in Sanskrit ; and the Voiced Aspirates occurred in a great number of words in the parent Indo-European language.

None of these sounds occur in pure Latin words ; but Breathed Aspirates existed in Greek at least down to the Christian era, and frequently appear in words borrowed from Greek into Latin, e.g. in names like *Philippus, Phoebus, Charon.* They must be carefully distinguished from the fricative sounds like Eng. *th,* Germ. *ch* (see §§ **38, 41**).

§ **51.** But the Aspirates, both in Greek words and in Latin words borrowed from Greek, passed into Fricatives some time in the course of the Roman Empire, so that the first syllable of *Philippus* came to be pronounced as it still is in English, and so *ph* came to be only another way of writing *f.* But in Greek, before the Christian era, the Breathed Aspirates ϕ, θ, and χ were pronounced like *ph* in Eng. *uphill*, *th* in Eng. *boat-house*, *kh* in Eng. *pack-horse*.

English and Latin h, *Greek* '

§ **52.** The sound which is denoted by the letter *h* is a slight rustle of Breath, which can hardly be heard unless a Vowel or Liquid immediately follows. A rustle of this sort can be produced by a very slight rubbing of the current of Breath at almost any point. In English it is made by sending some Breath through the larynx while the Vocal Edges are in course of being stretched : so soon as they are stretched the following vowel sound begins.

§ **53.** The proper name for the sound of *h* is therefore what it is called in Greek, namely a ' rough breathing ' ; and it is unfortunate that it has popularly come to be called " the aspirate," since this word is used in Phonetics, as we have seen, to mean something different.

III. SOME PRE-HISTORIC CHANGES AND THEIR FRUITS

The Sounds of Pro-ethnic Indo-European

§ **54.** THE chief sounds which can be shown to have existed in words that descended from Indo-European into Latin are these :

> Vowels : *a, e, i, o, u, ə.*
> Liquids and Nasals : *r, l ; m, n.*

		Breathed	*Voiced*
Fricatives :	Dental	*s*	*z*
Plosives :	Velar	*q*	*g̗*
	Palatal	*k̂*	*ĝ*
	Dental	*t*	*d*
	Labial	*p*	*b*

Voiced Aspirates : *gh, ĝh, dh, bh.*

Besides these there were the Non-vowel Sonants (*r̥, l̥, m̥, n̥*) ; the Semi-vowels, Consonantal *i* and *u* (*i̯* and *u̯*) ; the Velar nasal *ŋ̑*, and the Palatal nasal *ñ*, all of which have been just described. Of the difference between the so-called " Pure Velars " and the other Velars something will be said in § **173**.

Most of these sounds except the Aspirates (§§ **174** ff.)

and the Non-vowel Sonants (§§ **197** and **207**), remained the same on passing into early Latin; their changes in Latin we shall see later on.

The Neutral Vowel

§ **55.** The I.Eu. neutral vowel *ə* (§ **29**) became *i* in Sanskrit, but *ă* in Greek and Latin, e.g. in Lat. *status* 'fixed,' Gr. στατός, compared with Sansk. *sthitás* 'placed, standing.'

The Sign :

§ **56.** A direct connection between two words is often conveniently expressed by the symbol : , which is used to mean 'in relation to.' Thus we may state the facts just mentioned by writing :

I.Eu. *ə* appears in I.Eu. **stətós* : Sans. *sthitás* : Gr. στατός : Lat. *status*.

These three words are identical, that is, they all go back to the same original. But the sign : denotes any direct kind of relation between two forms; for example we may write " *gero : gestus*," " *cado : concido*," " Eng. *man* : Eng. *men*," reading the sign as a short way of writing 'considered in relation to' or 'when compared with' or 'beside.'

Some early Phonetic Changes

§ **57.** Before studying the history of these sounds in Latin, it will help us to consider briefly two sets of changes which happened outside the separate history

of Latin, but which greatly affected the relations of
the sounds which we find existing in Latin to those
which we find in parallel words in the kindred languages.
For example we find (1) Lat. *māter* : Eng. *mother*

(2) Lat. *tentus* : Gr. τατός, Sans. *tatás* ' stretched '
all clearly related also to Gr. τείνω ' I stretch,' and
Lat. *tenor* ' stretch, continuance.'

Similar correspondences occur in a host of other
words.

§ 58. The first correspondence becomes clear as
soon as we know something of the phonetic changes
which happened in early, that is, pro-ethnic [1] Germanic
which are called G r i m m a n d V e r n e r ' s L a w.
The second group of words has been shaped by changes
caused by A c c e n t in the Indo-European parent
language. Both these sets of changes are easy to
understand and throw a great light on the history of
all the descendant languages. Grimm and Verner's
Law also depends partly upon the Indo-European
Accent ; and as it affected the Germanic languages
only, it will be best to state it first.

Grimm and Verner's Law in pro-ethnic Germanic

§ 59. In the Germanic branch before any of the
Germanic languages that we know (§ 8) had split off
from the rest, all the Plosives and Aspirates which had
been inherited from the parent Indo-European language
suffered phonetic changes which are often called ' the
Sound-shift.' These were first formulated in 1822 by
the German scholar Jacob Grimm who made the

[1] See § 3

famous collection of fairy-tales. His statement was completed by the Danish scholar Verner in 1875, who explained a mass of exceptions by discovering the second of the four rules which follow.

§ **60.** In early Germanic, probably at some time between 500 and 200 B.C., the following changes took place :

(1) All Breathed Plosives (unless preceded by s) became the corresponding Breathed Fricatives, p became f, t became þ (Eng. *th* in *thin*) and so on. Thus

f in Eng. *full*　corresponds to p in Lat. *plēnus*,
th in Eng. *thorn*　　,,　　　,,　t in Lat. *terō*,

and, since the Germanic Palatal Fricative became later merely h in English, h in Eng. *hund-red* corresponds to c in Lat. *centum*. But after s the Plosives were unchanged, as in Eng. *sta-nd* : Lat. *stā-re.*

(2) (*a*) These Breathed Fricatives remained when they came at the beginning of a word, as in the examples just given, or when they occurred immediately after a syllable bearing the Accent, as in the suffix -*th* which in English in such words as *youth, width*, corresponds to -*t*- in Latin in such words as *iuven-ta, senec-ta*. We know from Greek and Sanskrit that the syllable preceding this suffix was accented in the parent Indo-European language. So Eng. *mother, brother* [1] beside Gr. μήτηρ (older μᾱ́τηρ), φρᾱ́τηρ 'member of a group of families.'

(*b*) But when the Breathed Fricative stood before a vowel which itself bore the accent, the Breathed

---

[1] The -*th*- in these words was once the Breathed fricative (§ 41) as in *youth*, not Voiced as it has become in modern English.

Fricative became Voiced in early Germanic, and then generally became a Voiced Plosive ; so in this case we have regularly Eng. *b, d, g,* corresponding to I.Eu. and Lat. *p, t, k.*

Thus the Eng. *-d* of participles and adjectives (as in *loved,* or *moneyed*) comes from the original *-t-* which is preserved in the Lat. ending *-tus* (§ 232), Greek *-τός,* Sans. *-tás* ; Greek and Sanskrit keep the original accent on the ending. So the *-d-* in Eng. *gard-en* comes from the *-t-* which is preserved in Gr. χορτός, ' cleared space,' Lat. *hortus.* So the *-d-* in Cumberland-English *fader* represents correctly the *-τ-* before the accented syllable in Gr. πατήρ, Sans. *pitā ;* the *-th-* in southern English is due to an analogical assimilation to the *-th-* in *mother.*

(3) The Indo-European Voiced Aspirates became in Germanic Voiced Fricatives and these, as we have just seen, became Voiced Plosives.

Thus Eng. *b* in *to bear* corresponds to Sans. *bh* in *bhar-āmi,* Gr. φέρω, Lat. *fero* (§ 175), all meaning ' I bear.'

Eng. *d* in *dare, durst* answers to Sans. *dh* in *dhárṣati* ' he dares,' Gr. θ in θάρσος ' boldness.'

Eng. *g* in *garden* answers to I.Eu. *ĝh* which appears as χ in Gr. χορτός and *h* in Lat. *hortus.*

(4) The Voiced Plosives became Breathed.

Thus Eng. *p* in *thorpe* corresponds to Lat. *b* in *trabs,* ' beam for building.'

,,	,,	*t*	,,	*(to) tow*	,,	,, ,,	*d* ,, *dūco,* ' I draw, lead.
,,	,,	*c*	,,	*(bishop)-ric*	,,	,, ,,	*g* ,, *rēgnum,* ' king- ' dom

§ 61. These four sets of changes imply so great an alteration in the sounds of the original language that scholars are now agreed in thinking that they came about because the Indo-European language was acquired by a people originally quite strange to it, probably in consequence of some great conquest or invasion in Central and Northern Europe between the dates mentioned at the beginning of the last section. But whether Indo-European was the language of the invading or the invaded people has not yet been fully determined.

The changes just described are generally described by German scholars as ' the first Sound-shift ' ; because many hundred years later, when High German was separated from the other Germanic languages, a ' second Sound-shift ' happened which created the most important differences between the consonants of Modern German and those of the other Germanic languages such as Danish, Dutch and English. These changes however do not come within the scope of this book.

Accent

§ 62. By an A c c e n t we mean the degree of prominence in speaking given to one particular syllable above the other syllables of the same word or phrase. Thus in Eng. *merrily* the first syllable, in *abandon* the second syllable, in *ascertain* the third syllable has the Accent of the word ; in *hear me,* or *down with it* the first syllable has the Accent of the phrase ; in *be quiet !* the second syllable.

Enclitics and Proclitics

§ **63.** In all such phrases the unaccented words that come after the accented syllable are said to be E n c l i t i c (*me* and *with it* in the first two phrases): those that come before it are called P r o c l i t i c (*be* in *be quíet*).

Stress Accent

§ **64.** But there are two ways in which this prominence of a syllable can be made audible in speech.

The first is by pronouncing the accented syllable with greater f o r c e than the rest, as we do in English. This is called a S t r e s s Accent, or an E x s p i r a- t o r y Accent, because it depends on the force of our exspiration.

Musical Accent

§ **65.** But in some languages the Accented syllable is pronounced not necessarily with more force, but upon a h i g h e r n o t e than the others, the Vocal Edges (§§ **24–27**) being more tightly stretched while the Sonant part of that syllable is being made. This is called a T o n e Accent, or M u s i c a l Accent.

In Ancient Greek, in Sanskrit, and in the latest period of pro-ethnic Indo-European this Musical accent prevailed. It still survives in Lithuanian, which in this and some other respects is the most primitive of the spoken languages of modern Europe. But in some period earlier than the latest of the undivided Indo-

European language, the Accent must have carried a strong Stress (see § **69**).

Change of Character in Accent

§ **66.** The character of the Accent may change in a language. Thus in Greek in the 5th Century B.C. it was certainly Musical; but by the 2nd Century A.D., if not earlier, it had certainly become Exspiratory as it is in Modern Greek; hence came the lengthening of the vowel in the accented syllable, frequent in even Attic inscriptions of the 2nd Century A.D. (e.g. Σώλωνος instead of Σόλωνος C.I.A. iv. 11, written between 174 and 178 A.D.), and occurring much earlier in Greek papyri from Egypt. In Modern Greek accented vowels are regularly long.

Character of Latin Accent

§ **67.** In Latin the Accented syllable was pronounced with greater Stress, but it is possible that there was some raising of the Tone also in the language of polite society. But in the everyday speech of the camps from which all the Romance languages outside Italy arose, the Stress accent was very strong. This was the cause of the remarkable contractions and mutilations that appear in some of these languages, especially in French; for example in such a word as *cité* from Lat. *cīvitătem*, where the stress accent on the syllable *-tā-* (see § **85** (4)) has helped

     (1) to suppress the syllable *-vi-*,

     (2) to shorten the *i* of *cī-*,

     (3) to suppress the final syllable altogether.

Written Signs of Accent

§ 68. Here it is well to note that the ' acute ' sign is properly only used to mark an accented syllable ; and the ' circumflex ' (^ or ⌢ or ~) is properly used only in languages with a Musical accent, and then to mark a syllable in which the tone rises on the first half of the syllable and falls on the second half, as in Gr. τοῦτο.

Unfortunately these convenient signs have come to be used in writing many languages to denote not Accent at all, but merely a particular quality or quantity of vowel ; as in Fr. *passé, cité* to mark a particular kind of *e* ; or as in Fr. *hâter* to mark a long vowel.   And still more unluckily these actual signs are called ' accents ' although in fact they do not in such cases denote Accent at all.

ABLAUT

§ 69. In some period of the Indo-European parent language the Stress-accent upon one syllable robbed a preceding or following syllable of much of its quantity ; words like Lat. *dūco* (older *déuco) ' I lead,' *fīdo*, older *feido* ' I trust,' show in their first syllable what is called the N o r m a l form of the root ; and this was preserved because in these verbs that syllable was accented in Indo-European.   But there are words from the same roots, like *dux, ducis* ' leader,' *fidēs* ' trust,' which show a short form of the root, containing only *ŭ* or *ĭ* instead of *eu* and *ei ;* and this short or ' Weak ' form arose not in Latin but in Indo-European in words which had originally contained the Normal form of root but in which the Accent in that period fell on the following syllable, and had thus reduced the root-syllable to a Weak form.

We find similar variation due ultimately to the same cause in suffixes (§ **226–243**), as in *-ter- -tr-*, *-en-* and *-n-*, *-meno-* and *-mno-*.

§ **70.** The commonest case of this weakening of syllables through their coming to stand in an unaccented position is the Participle in *-tós*, where, as we have seen in § **60** (2) (*b*), the suffix always bore the accent. Hence e.g. the partc. of I.Eu. **ten-i̯ō* ' I stretch ' (Gr. τείνω, Lat. *tendo*) became not **ten-tós* but **tn̥tós* which appears in Gr. τατός, Sans. *tatás*, for in Greek and Sanskrit *n̥* and *m̥* both became *a*. In Latin however *n̥* always became *en*, so the Latin form is *tentus*. The Verbal Nouns ending with the suffix *-ti-*, which was always accented, also show the Weak form of the root, as Gr. φάτις, from the root of Lat. *fāma*, Gr. φᾱμί, φημί, or Gr. πίσ-τις beside πείθω, or Lat. *ratis* beside *rē-ri* ' to think ' (§ **216**).

§ **71.** From roots whose Normal form contained *ā*, *ē*, or *ō*, the Weak form in Indo-European had the neutral vowel *ə* which became short *a* in Latin (§ **55**). This explains such groups of forms as the following :

Root *dhē-* (sometimes in a longer form *dhēk̑-*) ' to make, put,' Gr. τί-θη-μι, ἔ-θηκ-α.
 : Sans. *da-dhā-mi*.
 : Lat. *fēcī* beside *facio*.

Root *stā-* ' to stand, make to stand,' Gr. (Doric)
  ἴ-στᾱ-μι.
  : Sans. *ti-ṣṭhā́-mi.*
  : Lat. *stā-re, stā-men* beside *status.*
Root *dō-* ' to give,' Gr. δί-δω-μι.
  : Sans. *da-dā́-mi.*
  : Lat. *dō-num* beside *datus,* and also *damus,*
    datis, dabo.

§ 72. There seems to have been under some special
conditions a still further weakened stage in which even
the -ə- completely vanished : Sans. *devattás* ' god-
given ' stands for **deiu̯o-d-tós ;* and Lat. *vici-ss-im*
' by giving in turn ' seems to show the same grade
of the same root with -ss- from -d-t- (§ 166) ; on -im
see § 269.

§ 73. The changes just described happened in a
period of the I.Eu. parent speech long before any of
the descendant languages had split off. But at a later
period, not long before the earliest separation, perhaps
as recently as 3000 or even 2000 B.C., the character
of the Accent had become more musical (§ 65). This
seems to have produced quite a different kind of effect
on the vowels of unaccented syllables. These were
not shortened or crushed out as unaccented vowels
had been in the Stress-accent period, but c h a n g e d
i n q u a l i t y. Thus -e- (and probably -a-) in a syllable
preceding the accented syllable became -o-. This
affected a great number of words which had been
created in the language after the period of Stress-
accent was over. Thus from I.Eu. **léĝo* ' I tell,
count ' were formed abstract nouns **loĝā́* and **loĝós*

' telling, counting '; from *tégo ' I cover,' an abstract
noun *togā́ ' covering '; from *bhéi̯dhō ' I trust '
(or transitively ' I make to trust ') which became
Lat. fīdō, the reduplicated perfect *bhébhoi̯dha ' I have
trusted ' which became Gr. πέποιθα. These -o- forms
are said to contain the D e f l e c t e d form of the root.

§ **74.** Thus we get sets of forms such as these
appearing in separate languages :

Normal form of root.	Deflected form of root.
Lat. *ago*, Gr. ἄγω ' I drive '	: Gr. ὀγ-μός ' furrow.'
Lat. *tego* ' I cover '	: Lat. *toga* ' a man's robe.'
Gr. δέμω ' I build '	: Gr. δόμος, Lat. *domus* ' house.'
Gr. λείπω ' I leave '	: Gr. λέλοιπα ' I have left.'
Old Lat. *feido*, Gr. πείθομαι ' I trust, am persuaded '	: Gr. πέποιθα, ' I have learnt to trust,' Lat. *foed-us* ' pledging of trust, covenant.'

(The changes of the consonants in this last set will
be explained in §§ **174** ff., **182.**)

§ **75.** The examples given, e.g. Gr. δόμος, show that
even in Greek the Indo-European accent had been
shifted in many words from the place in the word
which it had had in Indo-European ; and we shall see
(Chap. V) that the place of the Accent was completely
changed in Latin. Nevertheless the forms produced by
the old system remained in the separate languages,
sometimes isolated like bits of wreckage left high and
dry on the beach by the tide.

§ **76.** But the different branches of Indo-European
started on their separate development already possessing a great number of sets of words thus produced.

The words in each set were linked together by their meaning but showed their different types, those with the N o r m a l, those with the W e a k, and those with the D e f l e c t e d form of root. These types are called G r a d e s   o f   A b l a u t. A b l a u t is a convenient German name (literally : 'variation of sound') for the connexion between the Normal forms on the one hand and the Weak and Deflected forms on the other.

§ 77. Now these new forms, though they had arisen by unconscious phonetic changes, had come to be associated with special kinds of meaning, e.g.

Normal.	Weak.	Deflected.
I.Eu. *ten-i̯ō 'I stretch'	*tn̥tós 'stretched'	*tétone 'he has stretched.'
		*tonós 'a stretching.'
Gr. τείνω	τατός	τέτονε, τόνος.
Lat. tendo, tenor	tentus	
I.Eu. *leiq-ō 'I leave'	*éliqom 'I left'	*leloiqe 'he has left.'
	*liq-tós 'left'	*loiqós 'remaining.'
Gr. λείπω	ἔ-λιπον	λέλοιπα, λοιπός.
Lat.	re-lic-tus	

Thus the Weak form came to be felt as proper to the partc. in -tos and the Deflected form as proper to the Perfect Active (in the Singular) and to derived Nouns or Adjectives of what we call the First and Second Declensions; compare also the examples in §§ 71, 73 and 74.

Hence it is true to say that though the phonetic changes which had first produced the Grades of Ablaut had long ceased, yet the system of Ablaut so created had become charged with grammatical meanings, and new forms could be made upon the pattern so established, and were made, in fact, in many of the branches of Indo-European.

§ **78.** In English, we have verbs conjugated like this

Present tense	Participle	Past tense
sink	*sunken*	*sank*

which represent the type; for the *-in-* of the English present has come regularly from an earlier *-en-*; the *-un-* of the Partc. represents a Sonant like the η of I.Eu. **tṇtós;* and the *-a-* of the past tense has come regularly from an earlier *-o-*.

§ **79.** Besides these three common Grades, there were others which appear in Latin only in a few forms. We have the Lengthened grade of the suffix-syllable in Gr. Nominatives like πα-τήρ ' father ' and ποι-μήν ' shepherd,' beside the Normal form in the Acc. πα-τέρ-α, ποι-μέν-α, and the Weak form in the Gen. πα-τρ-ός and in derivatives like πά-τρ-ιος ' belonging to one's father,' ποι-μν-ή ' flock.' The same variety appears also in the Deflected forms, e.g. in the compound Adj. Nom. εὐπάτωρ ' well-sprung,' εὔφρων ' well-minded, cheerful ' beside the Accusatives εὐπάτορα, εὔφρονα just as in the simple nouns πατήρ, πατέρα and φρήν, φρένα ' mind.' Examples of the Lengthened forms appear in Old Lat. Nominatives like *patēr* (later *pater*, § **95**); and the Lengthened Deflected forms appear in Nouns of the Agent in *-tōr*, later *-tor*; or of the suffix *-es-* : *-os-* in abstract Nouns like *odōs*, later *odor* (§ **243**). In both these types of Nouns the long vowel was carried by Analogy all through the declension (Acc. *monitōrem*, etc.), though by the time of Cicero the final syllable of the Nom. had been shortened (§ **130**). Contrast with these the Weakened form *-tr-* on which the corresponding Feminines are based, e.g. Acc. *moni-tr-īc-em* (§ **231**). In nouns like *homo* from older *homō* (§ **95**) the Strengthened Deflected form appears in the Nom. Sing. But in some words, such as *sermō* ' conversation,' *tēmō* ' pole of a chariot,' the Strengthened form spread through all the cases.

IV. THE SOUNDS AND ACCENT OF CICERO'S LATIN

§ **80.** WE are now prepared to study the chief changes of sound that happened in Latin after it had become a separate language. But for clearness' sake it is well to begin by observing what the sounds of the language actually were, and how the language was accented, in the time of Cicero, that is, after most of the changes which we shall have to study in what follows had been completed.

SCHEME OF LATIN PRONUNCIATION

§ **81.** The following list of Latin sounds is taken from the table issued by the authority of the Classical Association.

Vowels.

ā (*prātum*), as **a** in *father*.

ă (*răpit*), the same sound shortened as **a** in a*ha*.

ē (*mēta*), as **e** in *prey*, Fr. **é** as in *blé*.

ĕ (*frĕta*), as **e** in *fr͜͝*

ī (*fīdo*), as **ee** in *fe*   Fr. **ie** in *am*ie.

ĭ (*plĭco*), as **i** in *fit*.

ō (*nōtus*), as **o** in *no*   nearer Italian **o** in *Roma*.

ŏ (*nŏta*), as **o** in *not*,   . **o** in *botte*.

D

ū (*tūto*), as **oo** in *sh**oo**t*, Ital. **u** in *l**u**na* (not as *u* (*yew*)
    in *acute*).

ŭ (*cŭtis*), as **u** in *f**u**ll* (not as *u* in *accurate*, nor as *u*
    in *shun*).

§ **82.** *Diphthongs.*

The sounds of the diphthongs may be arrived at
by running the two component vowel-sounds rapidly
together, the second being pronounced lightly. The
most important are :

ae (*portae*) = $\widehat{a+e}$, nearly as **ai** in *Is**ai**ah* (broadly
    pronounced), Fr. *ém**ai**l* (not as *a* in *late*).

au (*aurum*) = $\widehat{a+u}$, as **ou** in *h**ou**r*, as Ital. **au** in
    *fl**au**to*.

oe (*poena*) = $\widehat{o+e}$, nearly as **oi** in *b**oi**l* (not as *ee* in
    feet, nor as *a* in *late*).

The following diphthongs occur more rarely :

ui (*huic, cui*) = $\widehat{u+i}$, as Fr. **oui.**

eu (*heu*) = $\widehat{e+u}$, nearly as English **ew** in *n**ew**.*

ei (*ei* interjection, or *Pompēī*, voc. of *Pompeius*)
    = $\widehat{e+i}$, as **ey** in *gr**ey*** (not as *i* in *dine*).

The recommendations for *ae* and *oe* were based
mainly on practical considerations, since it has been
found by experience that this pronunciation is of
great convenience. It is certain that this was the
pronunciation given them in early Latin, and that
they were still clearly distinct from the long *ē* in
the time of Cicero, though their precise sound then
is difficult to determine.

§ **83.** *Consonants.*

c, g are always hard.

c (*cepi, accepi*), as **c** in c*at*.

g (*gero, agger*), as **g** in g*et*.

So even before i.

c (*facio*), as **c** in c*at* (not as *s*, nor as *sh*).

g (*tegit*), as **g** in g*et*.

ng (*tangit*), as **ng** in fi*nger* (not as in *hanging*).

t is always hard, even before i.

t (*fortia, ratio*), as **t** in *native*.

s is always a breathed, dental sound.

s (*sub, rosa, res, sponsio*), as **s** in s*it*, spon*s*or, **ce** in ra**ce** (not as in *rose* or *raise*, nor as in *conclusions*).   Similarly when compounded ;

x (*exul*) = **ks**, as in e*xtract*,

bs (*urbs*) = **ps** (not *bz*).

i and u consonantal.

i̯ (j), e.g. *jacio*, as **y** in y*ou* (not as *j* in *Jack*).

u̯ (v), e.g. *volo*, practically as **w** in w*e*, Fr. **ou** in ou*i* (not as *v* in *very*, see § **153**).

qu (*qui, quod*), as **qu** in qu*een*.

gu (*unguere*), as **gu** in a*nguish*, **gw** in **Gw**endolen.

r was always trilled, even in the middle and at the end of words, e.g. in ra**r**us ; pa**r**ma, datu**r** (not as in English *palmer, hatter*).

Double consonants, e.g. vac-*ca*, pul-*lus*, were pronounced separately, as they regularly are in Italian, or as in English *book-keeper, well let.*

§ **84.** For a fuller explanation of this statement and comments on one or two special points (such as the sound of the diphthongs *ae, oe*, of final -*m*, and of *ph, th, ch* in words borrowed from Greek) the student is referred to Messrs. Arnold and Conway's *Restored Pronunciation of Latin and Greek* (Pitt Press) or to Messrs. Hale and Buck's *Latin Grammar* (Messrs. Ginn and Co.). Something has been said of *ph, th, ch* in §§ **50** ff. above.

The Latin Accent

§ **85.** The rules which state the place of the Accent in Latin words in the time of Cicero are these :

(1) M o n o s y l l a b l e s are accented, unless they are Enclitics like *-que, -ve,* or Proclitics (§ **63**) like Prepositions which were pronounced in combination with the word which followed them ; thus a phrase like *in ménsam* has only one accent.

Disyllabic Prepositions, however, retain an accent of their own, though it was generally a weaker accent than that of the word which followed : *ínter hóstes* had a stronger accent on the syllable *hós-* than on the syllable *ín-*.

(2) D i s y l l a b i c words were always accented on the first syllable, as *ménsa, páter, ámat.* Some disyllables, however, had become Enclitics like *quoque, enim* and generally *mihi, tibi, sibi* and some other pronominal forms ; then they threw back their accent as in *núnc-quoque, nón-enim,* and often *díc mihi.*

(3) The only exceptions to the rule just stated are words which have lost a final syllable by elision, as in *audín* ' do you hear ? ' from *audís-ne ;* these generally kept the Accent in the same place as it had held when the words were Trisyllabic. For *viden* see § **95.**

(4) In words of three or more syllables the place of the Accent depends upon the quantity of the Penult, a name derived from *paene ultima (syllaba)* ' the almost-last syllable.'

If the Penult is long, it takes the Accent, as *amămus, amăbam,* but *amābămus, amāvérunt; volúptas,* but *voluptătis.* If the Penult is short, the Accent is on the Ante-Penult, *aúdio, óptimus, pétere, requiéscere.*

A syllable of course is long when it contains either a long vowel or a diphthong, or a vowel followed by a consonant which has another consonant following it. Thus in a word like *perditus* the first syllable is long although the -*e*- in it is itself a short vowel.

(5) In words which contain two or more syllables before the Accented syllable, there is generally a weaker accent on one of these preceding syllables ; in that part of the word this secondary accent is placed just as the chief accent would have been if that part had been a separate word ;

cónquiéscere, cónturbăbimus, éxagităre, but *ingúrgităre, exaúctōrăre,* where " denotes the chief, ' the secondary accent.

(6) The place of the chief accent is often changed by a following Enclitic ; *aúctor,* but *auctórque, auctórem,* but *aúctōrémque ;* so *audísti* but *aúdistĭn(e).*

(7) So in colloquial phrases like the Vocative *voluptăs mea* ' my delight, my darling,' the addition of *mea* has pulled the accent of the phrase on to the last syllable of *voluptās* (on this see also § **95** below).

V. EARLIER BEHAVIOUR OF THE LATIN ACCENT

§ 86. We have now seen something of the nature of the Accent in the Indo-European language just before the Italic branch separated from the others ; and also in the Latin of Cicero's time. The course of its development in between these two epochs has been cleared up by recent study ; and as the facts throw great light on the derivation of a great many Latin words it will be well to state them briefly here.

§ 87. In pro-ethnic Italic, that is before Latin and other dialects (**§ 9**) had become separate, the chief Accent of every word was shifted to the first syllable, no matter what its place had been in Indo-European.

To this was due the degradation of the vowels (**§ 120**) in such forms as *acceptus*, from **ád-captos*, *contingo* from **cón-tango*.

Accent in Plautine Latin

§ 88. By the 3rd Century (300–200) B.C., this system had given way to one which limited the place of the word-accent to one of the last four syllables of the word, and made it depend upon the quantities of the second, third, and fourth syllables from the end. The following are the rules (determined by Prof. Chas. Exon) which describe the system as it was in the time of Plautus (say about 200 B.C.).

(1) If the Penult was long, it bore the accent (*amābāmus*).

(2) If the Penult was short, then

    (*a*) if the Ante-penult was long, it bore the accent (*amābimus*).

    (*b*) if the Ante-penult as well as the Penult was short, then (i) if the Ante-ante-penult was long, then the accent was on the Ante-penult (*amīcítia*) ; but (ii) if the Ante-ante-penult was also short it bore the accent (*cólumine, puéritia*).

Syncope in Latin

§ **89.** With these facts are linked what may be called Exon's Laws of S y n c o p e, i.e. of contraction causing the loss of a whole syllable. The first of these may be stated as follows :

In pre-Plautine Latin in all words or word-groups of four or more syllables whose chief accent was on a long syllable, a short unaccented medial vowel was syncopated : **cóntetulī, *contetíndī* (§ **293**) became *contulī, contendī ; *quínquedecem* became **quínqdecem* and thence *quíndecim* (for the -*im* see § **122**) ; **súpsemere* became **súpsmere* and that *sūmere* (on -*psm*- see § **191**) ; **súrregere, *surregémus* and the like became *súrgere, surgémus,* and the rest of the verb followed ;

so *supo-téndo became sub-tendo,[1] *āridére, *avidére (from āridus, avidus) became ārdére, audére. In phrases also similar changes arose ; probably válidē mágnus became váldē-mágnus, exterā víam became extrā viam, áqua cálida became aqua-cálda.

§ 90. But the influence of cognate forms often interfered ; posterídiē became postrídiē ; but in posterórum, posterārum the short syllable was restored by the influence of the trisyllabic cases like pósterā to which the law did not apply. Conversely the Nom. *āridor, which, as it had only three syllables, would not have been contracted, followed the form of ārdórem (from *āridórem), ārdére, and the like, which to start with had four.

§ 91. The same change produced the monosyllabic forms nec, ac, neu, seu, from neque, etc., before consonants, since they had often no strong accent of their own, but were commonly pronounced in one breath with the following word, neque tantum becoming nec tantum and the like. So in Plautus (and probably always in spoken Latin) the words nemp(e), ind(e), ill(e) were regularly pronounced as monosyllables.

§ 92. It is possible that the frequent (but far from universal) syncope of final short syllables in Latin (especially before -s, as in mēns which may stand for both *menos and *mentis and represent both Greek μένος ' spirit, force ' and Sanskrit matís, I.Eu. *mn̥tís, Eng.

---

[1] On the -b- which arose before certain sounds see **§ 156.** Before t and s, however, it was pronounced p and often correctly so written.

mind) is due also to this law operating on such com-
binations as *bona mēns* and the like ; but the conditions
of this change have not yet been clearly shown. That
some such change, however, was regular in early Latin
appears probable from the many examples of words
which in other languages appear as -*o*- stems but which
in Latin have been shifted to the consonantal declension ; for example *pons* ' causeway, bridge ' beside
Gr. πόντος ' strait, sea ' (both meaning properly ' a
crossing '—cf. Sansk. *panthan*-' road ') ; and *glans*
beside Gr. βάλανος both meaning ' acorn, nut ' (see § **170**).
In many words the effects of this phonetic change, if
it took place, must have been very greatly modified
by analogy.

§ **93.** The second law states the syncope which
took place later than the time of Plautus.

In post-Plautine spoken Latin before Cicero's time
words accented on the Ante-ante-penult suffered
syncope of the short syllable following the accented
syllable ; *bálineae* became *bálneae, puéritia* became
puértia, cólumine tégimine, etc., became *cúlmine tégmine*,
etc. (beside the trisyllabic Nominatives *cólumen,
tégimen*), except in the one case described in the next
section.

§ **94.** When the short vowel was *e* or *i* or *u* followed
by another vowel (as in *párietem, múlierem, Púteoli*)
the word was not contracted, but the accent was shifted
to the Penult, which at a later stage of the language
became lengthened. Thus late Latin *pariétem* gave
Italian *paréte*, Fr. *paroi ;* late Latin *Puteóli* gave
Italn. *Pozzuōli*. The restriction of the accent to the

three last syllables was completed by these changes
which did away with all the cases in which it had stood
on the fourth syllable from the end.

Brevis Brevians

§ **95.** Next must be mentioned another phonetic
change, also dependent upon Accent, which had come
about before the time of Plautus, the law long known
as the *Brevis Brevians* which may be stated as follows :
A syllable long by nature or position, and preceded
by a short syllable, was itself shortened if the accent of
the word fell immediately before or immediately after
it,—that is, on the preceding short syllable or on the
next following syllable. The set of syllables need not
be in the same word, but must be as closely connected
in utterance as if they were. Thus *mŏ́dō* became
módŏ, *ŏdōr* became *ódŏr*, *vŏluptătem* became *vŏlŭ'tătem*,
est in *quĭ́d est ?* became a short syllable (either the *s* or
the *t* or both being only faintly pronounced).

§ **96.** It is clear that a great number of Inflexional
syllables which had been shortened by this Phonetic
Change, must have had their quantity immediately
restored on the pattern of the same inflexion when it
occurred in words not of this particular shape ; thus,
for instance, the long vowel of *ămā* is due to that in
other verbs (*pulsā*, *agitā*) not of iambic shape. So
Ablatives like *modō*, *sonō* got back their -ō as we have
seen (§ 15), though in Adverbs like *modo* ' only,' *quōmodo*
' how ' the shortened form remained. Conversely the
shortening of the final -*a* in the Nom. Sing. Fem.
of the *a*-declension (contrast *lūna* with Gr. χώρᾱ)

was due to the influence of common forms like *ĕă, bŏnă, mălă,* which had come under the Law because they were disyllables with their first syllable short.

§ **97.** These processes had far-reaching effects on Latin Inflexion. The chief of these was the establishment of the type of Conjugation known as the *capio-*class. All these verbs were originally inflected like *audio ;* but the accident of their short root-syllable (in such early forms as **fúgīs, *fugītūrus *fugīsétis* which later on became *fúgĭs, fugĭtūrus fugĕrétĭs* [1]) brought great parts of their paradigm under this Law, and the rest followed suit ; but true forms like *fugīre, cupīre, morīrī* never altogether died out of the spoken language ; St. Augustine, for instance, confesses in 387 A.D. (Epist. iii. 5) that he does not know whether *cupi* or *cupiri* is the Pass. Inf. of *cupio ;* hence Italn. *fuggire* ' to flee,' *morīre* ' to die,' Fr. *fuir, mourir.*

[1] On the *-r-* of *fugerētis* see § **186** ; on the *-e-* before the *-r-,* § **99** (2).

VI. THE LIFE-HISTORY OF LATIN SOUNDS

CHANGES OF VOWELS AND DIPHTHONGS IN LATIN

98. SOME of these changes happened i n d e -
p e n d e n t l y of the effects of A c c e n t; others
took place only in u n a c c e n t e d syllables.

Changes not connected with Accent

The most important of these may be briefly stated
here.

§ **99.** *ĭ* became *ĕ* under the following conditions :

(1) When it was final, as in *ant-e* beside Gr. *ἀντί* (both
the Locative Case of a Noun closely akin to Eng. *end*
and so meaning ' at the end of ') ; *trīste* beside *trīsti-s*
contrasted with Greek neuters in -*ι*, e.g. *ἴδρι*, from *ἴδρις*
' wise.' So too the final -*e* of the Infin. Act. (e.g. *regere*)
came from the -*ĭ* of the Locative, just as in the Ablatives
which were properly Locatives, e.g. *genere*, ' in race,
by race.'

(2) Before -*r*- which has arisen from -*s*- (§ **186**) as
in *cineris* compared with *cinis, cinisculus ; serō* from
*si-sō a reduplicated Present from the root *sē-*, which
appears in *sē-men* (like *si-sto*, from *stā-*, §§ **71, 282**).

50

§ 100. ĕ became ĭ when

(1) It was followed by a Palatal or Velar Nasal (§ **48**), as in *tingo* earlier *tengo, Gr. τέγγω ' I moisten ' ; *quinque*, earlier *quenque, cf. Gr. πέντε (§ **155**).

(2) Or by a Palatal or Velar plosive which was followed by a nasal : *dignus*, from earlier *dec-no-s ' becoming, fitting ' (cf. *decet*) ; *signum* from *seq-nom (cf. *sequor*) ' something to follow up, a mark.'

§ 101. That Lat. -*g*- before -*n*- was pronounced like Eng. -*ng* is probable from the spellings *ignārus, ignōtus, cognōsco* where the nasal of *in*- or *com*- was probably heard (though not written) before the -*g*- but of course assimilated to it, that is, having become a Palatal Nasal.

§ 102. ĕ became ĭ also under some other conditions such as the presence of ĭ or ī in the next syllable : *nĭhĭl* from *ne-hīlum, *nisi* from *ne-sī, *initium* from *en-itium. From such forms as well as from those in which *en*- had become *in*- before *c* or *g* (as in *incolo*, *ingero*) by the Assimilation of the Dental Nasal to the following Palatal Plosive and the rule given in § **100** (1) above and from other cases (e.g. those under § **122**) *in* came to be thought the proper form of the Preposition and it superseded *en* everywhere.

Change of el *to* ol

§ 103. *el* became *ol* if followed by any sound but *e, i* or *l*. Hence *volo, volt, voluntas* beside *velle, velim ;* in the Neut. noun whose stem was *heles*- ' green-stuff,' Gen. *heleris*, Plur. *helera*, the root-syllable became *hol*- in the Nom. Acc. Sing. *holus*, earlier *helos (§ 127), though the form holera also often appears on the pattern of the nom. sing. On olīva, oleum from *élaivom see § 143.

§ 104. o became u under certain conditions :

(1) When it came before -nc-, -ngu-, -mb-, as in Lat. uncus ' hook ' : Gr. ὄγκος ' hook, lump, burden.' Lat. unguis beside Gr. ὄνυξ ' nail ' ; Lat. umbo beside Gr. ὀμφα-λός ' boss of a shield.'

(2) When it came before l which is followed by any consonant save l, or before ll followed by a or o or u, as in Lat. sulcus : Gr. ὁλκός ' furrow '; ultra beside Old Lat. olle ; homullus from *homon-los (contrast collis, mollis where -ll- is followed by -i-). But -ur- which we find medially beside -or- (as in furnus beside formus and fornix) probably marks furnus and words like it as borrowed from some neighbouring dialect.

The same change in all final syllables ending in a consonant is best classed with the changes due to accent, see § 127.

NOTE.—The reason or reasons for the change in humus (contrast homo ' earthly creature, man '), numerus (cf. the root in Gr. νόμος ' custom, law,' νόμισμα ' coin ') and umerus (Gr. ὤμος) are not quite clear.

§ 105. Final -ŏ became -ĕ; e.g. in the 2nd Sing. Impv. Pass. and Depon., as Lat. sequere which is sound for sound equivalent to Gr. Attic ἕπου, Ion. ἕπεο (§ 169), earlier *ἕπεσο (§ 186). ipse and ille (if the -ll- comes from -ls-, § 196) contain the old Pron. *so ' that man,' ' he,' Gr. ὁ ' that, the,' Sans. sa ' he.'

§ **106.** When a long Vowel came to stand before another Vowel in the same word through loss of $i̯$ (§ **136**) or $u̯$ (§ **142**) it was always shortened ; thus the -eō of Intransitive verbs like *candeō, caleō* is for -ēi̯ō (where the ē is identical with the η in Gr. intransitive Aorists like ἐμάνη ' was mad,' ἐρρύη ' burst into flood ') and was thus confused with the ' Causative ' (better ' Factitive ') -ei̯ō which appears in verbs like *moneō* ' I make to think ') where the short e is original (§§ **136, 293**).

§ **107.** So when *audīvī* had become **audīī* (§ **142**), that became *audiī*. In certain cases the vowels were contracted as in *trēs, partēs* and the like with -ēs from -ei̯es, and probably in *amo* from **amāi̯ō*.

§ **108.** When a Voiced Plosive (*b, d,* or *g*) became Breathed by being assimilated to a following -*t*- or -*s*- a preceding short vowel was lengthened. Thus we have

> *scrīptus* from **scrĭb-to-s* (if we assume that it contained the Weak form of the root, § **70**).
> *vīsus,* earlier *vīssus* (§ **167**) from **vĭd-tos,* (§ **166**).
> *āctus, tāctus, rēctus, tēctus* from **ag-tos, *tag-tos, *reg-tos, *teg-tos.*

Contrast *captus* from **cap-tos (capio)*
> *fassus* from **fat-tos (fateor),* § **166**.
> *factus* from **fac-tos (facio).*

In all these last cases the vowel of the root-syllable remained short because the consonant which followed it did not become Breathed by assimilation, but had always been Breathed.

Hidden Quantities

§ **109.** As the first syllable of the last three examples (*captus, fassus, factus*) is long since it ends in a consonant which is followed by another, the student may reasonably ask how we know that the vowel of the syllable is itself short ; and, on the other hand, how we know that the vowels in the first syllables of *tāctus* and the like are themselves long.

We learn this from such evidence as the following :

(1) The fact that in compounds long vowels remained (§ **129**) but short vowels were often modified. Hence when we find *-e-* in compounds like *conceptus, confessus, confectus*, but *-a-* in *coactus, contactus* we see that the vowel was short to start with in the first set of words but long in the second set.

(2) In the derived Romance languages we find that Latin *ĭ* and *ī*, *ĕ* and *ē* developed into different sounds. Thus the *ī* of *scrīptus* produces *i* in Fr. *écrit ;* whereas, for instance, the *ĭ* of *mittere* produces the *-e-* of Fr. *mettre*. Again the *ē* of *tēctum* produces *oi* in Fr. *toit* (cf. § **10**); whereas the *ĕ* of e.g. *septem* produces the *ĕ* of *sept* (pronounced *sett*).

NOTE.—The quantity of a vowel which occurs in a syllable which is long because of the consonants which follow the vowel is said to be a H i d d e n   Q u a n t i t y.

§ **110.** All vowels became long when followed by *nf* or *ns* as in *īnfero, cōnsero* (contrast e.g. *intrā, contineo* where the vowel of the prepositions remained short), or in *tōnsus* beside *tondeo* (§ **166**) ; also before *nct, nx* as in *iūnctus, iūnxī* beside *iungo*.

Colloquial shortening of ū́

§ **111.** When an accented *ū* was followed by a single Breathed Plosive and that by a vowel, in colloquial pronunciation the *ū* became short but the Plosive was doubled. Hence we find vulgar forms like

succus, muccus, futtilis

instead of the more polite and earlier forms

sūcus, mūcus, fūtilis (§ **178**).

Changes of the Diphthongs independent of Accent

§ **112.** *eu* became *ou* in pro-ethnic Italic. Lat. *novus* : Gr. νέος, older νέϝος, Eng. *new*. Lat. *novem*, Umb. *novis* 'nine times' : Gr. ἐν-νέα (for ἐν-νέϝη §§ **70, 14**; but the origin of the first syllable of the Greek word has not yet been made clear).

§ **113.** *ou* whether original or from *eu*, when pronounced in one syllable, became -*ū*-, probably about 200 B.C., as in *dūcō*, Old Lat. *doucō*, Goth. *tiuhan* 'to draw,' Eng. *tow* (§ **60** (4)), I.Eu. **deu̯kō*.

§ **114.** *ei* became *ī* (as in *dīcō*, Old Lat. *deico* : Gr. δείκ-νῡμι, *fīdo* : Gr. πείθω : I.Eu. **bhei̯dhō*) just before the time of the poet Lucilius (say 130–100 B.C.) who prescribes the spellings *puerei* (Nom. Plur.), but *puerī* (Gen. Sing.). This indicates that the two forms were pronounced alike in his time, but that the traditional distinction in spelling had been more or less preserved. But after his time since the sound of *ei* was everywhere that of *ī*, *ei* is continually used merely to denote a long *ī*, even where as in *faxeis* instead of

E

faxīs, there never had been any diphthongal sound at
all (cf. § 23).

§ 115. In rustic Latin (Volscian and Sabine) *au*
became *ō* as in the vulgar *explōdere* ' to drive off the
stage by stamping,' *plōstrum* ' waggon,' both from
plaudo ' I beat, knock.' Hence arose interesting
doublets of meaning; *lautus* (the Roman form) 'elegant '
but *lōtus* ' washed '; *haustus* ' draught,' but *hōstus*
(Cato) ' the season's yield of fruit.' Cicero's enemy,
the demagogue Publius Clodius, belonged to the noble
patrician gens of the Claudii, but he deliberately
adopted the vulgar pronunciation and spelling of his
name, just as he arranged for himself to be made a
Plebeian by a special law.

§ 116. *oi* accented became *oe*, and finally *ū*, after
Plautus' time (though his spelling was modernised,
just as Shakespeare's has been), *ūnus* ' one ' : Old Lat.
oenos, cf. Gr. οἰνή ' ace '; Lat. *ūtor* : O. Lat. *oetor*,
originally meaning ' to get on, make one's way (by
means of something or some one),' cf. Gr. οἶτος ' path,
way.'

§ 117. But there was a small group of words in
which the old spelling was kept through their frequent
use in legal or religious documents where the traditional
spelling was strictly followed; *poena* ' a fine,' beside
the more colloquial *pūnio* ' I punish ' which was derived
from it. Similarly in *foedus* (neut.) ' treaty ' and in
the archaic and poetical *moenia* ' ramparts,' beside the
living words *mūnia* ' duties ' and *mūnus* ' privilege ';
in the historic name *Poeni* ' Carthaginians,' beside the
living and frequently used phrase *Pūnicum* (*bellum*).

This last example shows conclusively that the variation between $\bar{u}$ and *oe* is not due to any difference in the surrounding sounds.

§ **118.** *ai* became *ae*, and this in rustic dialects and in later Latin (2nd and 3rd Centuries A.D.) simply $\bar{e}$; from the root of Gr. αἴθω ' I burn ' comes Lat. *aedēs* (orig. ' the place for the fire '), in country Latin *ēdēs* (cf. § **177** (1)).

NOTE.—The diphthongs so far discussed are those which had a short vowel for their first component. Those whose first component was originally long ($\bar{a}\underset{\circ}{i}$, $\bar{e}\underset{\circ}{i}$, $\bar{o}\underset{\circ}{i}$; $\bar{a}\underset{\circ}{u}$, $\bar{e}\underset{\circ}{u}$, $\bar{o}\underset{\circ}{u}$) are in Latin only distinguishable from the others (*ai*, *au* and the rest) when they came at the end of words ; here they lost their second component altogether : compare in the dat. Gr. λόγῳ with Lat. *dominō* (Old Latin *-ōi*, see § **23**, Note i) ; and in the $\bar{a}$- and $\bar{e}$-Declensions we have in Old Latin datives like *Matutā*, *fidē*, though the endings were altered later to *ae* and *eī*. Lat. *duō*, *octō* beside Vedic Sansk. *dvāu* ' two,' *aṣṭāu* ' eight ' probably show a similar loss of $-\underset{\circ}{u}$.

VOWELS AND DIPHTHONGS IN UNACCENTED SYLLABLES

Short Vowels

§ **119.** The commonest changes of unaccented short Vowels in Medial syllables can be best shown by a few typical examples. From these it will be clear that according to the particular conditions :

> *a* sinks to *e* or *i* ;
> *e* remains or sinks to *i* ;
> *o* sinks to *u* or *i* ;
> *u* remains or sinks to *i*.

§ **120.** Before two consonants *a* becomes *e*, *e*

remains, o becomes u. *peperci*, perf. of *parco*, from
*péparcai (§ 297) ; *acceptus* from *ád-captos ; *ē-vello*,
contentus, show the *e* of *vello*, *tentus*, unchanged.
onustus from *ónos-tos ' burdened ' from *onus*, older
onos (neut.), see § 127.

§ 121. *a* and *o* before *r* become *e*, and *e* remains.
impero, for *ín-paro, lit. ' prepare upon (some one else),
arrange for (among some persons),' hence, as a military
term ' order some one to provide (*imperat sociis frumen-
tum*).' *vīve-rādīx* [1] ' living-root ' from *vivo-rādīx*. But
from *fero* we have *infero*, *confero*, etc.

Words like *comparo*, *adparo*, *perforo* were formed or
re-formed (§ 20) at a date after the changes of *ă* and *ŏ*
were over.

§ 122. *a, e, o, u* before single consonants other than
r and *l* become *i* (but see further § 127):

> *con-cino* from *cón-cano.
> *con-tineo* from *cón-teneo.
> *agri-cultura* from *agro-cultura.
> *hospitem* from *hósti-potem (§ 89).
> *genibus* from *genubus*.
> *legimus* older *légomos, cf. Gr. λέγο-μεν ' we
> lay it down, say.'

§ 123. But in s p e c i a l s u r r o u n d i n g s we
find *u* instead of *i*, e.g. before -*l*- : *Siculi* from Gr.
Σικελοί,

between *l* and *m* : *volumus* from *volomos,

before *p* or *b* followed by *a* or *o* : *occupo* for **ob-
capo* (contrast *ác-cipio* for *ád-capio).

---

[1] Later and less correctly written *vivi-radix;* cf. § 19.

before *m* : the variant spelling in words like

> *monumentum, monimentum,*
> *maxumus, maximus,*

perhaps points to a sound (like Germ. *ü*) midway
between *u* and *i*.

§ **124.** Similarly *a* or *e* instead of *i* : before *l* with
adjacent *a* : *calamus, alacer* (not *-im-, -ic-*) ; with
adjacent *e* : *hebetis,* gen. of *hebes ; neglego* beside
diligo, both from *lego*.

§ **125.** But in these last two examples, and in many
others, it is hard to be sure that the original vowel
has not been merely restored by Re-formation (§ **20**).

§ **126.** The compounds of *iacio* take a peculiar
form in the Present and the tenses derived from it,
abicio, conicio, reicio and so on, according to the spelling
which is regular in the inscriptions and in our best
manuscripts.   But in verse the first syllable is always
long (*ābicit*) and the compound with *dis-* is sometimes
spelt *dissicio*.   Some mediaeval scribes wrote regularly
abiecio, etc. ; but neither this nor *abiicio,* etc., are
warranted by inscriptions of the Ciceronian or of the
Augustan period.   It would seem that the sound
must have differed little from what in English we
should write *abyic-,* and yet not have been quite
identical with that.   It is one of the few cases in Latin
in which we have not evidence to determine the ancient
sound with complete precision.

-e- *and* -o- *in final Syllables*

§ **127.** Inscriptions of the 4th or 3rd Century B.C. which show original -*os* and -*es*, -*om*, -*ont*, in final syllables (e.g. *Veneres* gen. sing., *navebos* abl. plur., *opos* and *pocolom* nom. sing., *co(n)sentiont*, 3rd Pers. Plur.) compared with the usual -*is*, -*us*, -*um*, -*unt* of the 2nd and 1st Centuries B.C., give us roughly the date of these changes, which must have been later than 300 B.C. ; but final -*os*, -*om* remained after -*u*- (and *v*) down to 50 B.C. as in *servos* (see § **146**).

-ri- *and* -ro- *in Medial and Final Syllables*

§ **128.** Both accented and unaccented -*rĭ*- and -*rŏ*- became -*er*- in early Latin or pro-ethnic Italic both in Medial and Final Syllables : *ter* from **ters* and that from **tris* (Gr. τρίς), *incertus* from **éncritus*, *ager*, *ācer* from **ágros*, **ắcris;* where -*ers* became first -*err* (§ **190**) and then -*er*. The feminine *ācris* was restored by the analogy of other adjectives like *trīstis ;* but the masc. *ācer* was protected by the analogy of the parallel masc. forms of the -*o*- declension like *tener, niger* (from **teneros, *nigros*). Some words, however, show a re-formed nom. in -*rus* (*prosperus, īnferus, ferus*).

Long Vowels

§ **129.** Long Vowels generally remained unchanged as in *compāgo, condōno*. But -*ē*- became -*ī*- in *inquilīnus, convīcium, suspīcio* from **convēc-, *suspēc-* because of the

-i- in the adjacent syllable (*-ium*) ; *suspēc-* for **subspēc-* contains the lengthened form of the root seen in *speculum, spec-to ; con-vēc-* a lengthened form (§ 79) of the root seen in *vōx, vōc-is,* which has the lengthened Deflected form.

§ 130. Long vowels were shortened before final *-r* and final *-t,* e.g. in the ending *-tor* (earlier *-tōr*) and *-at* (*agitat, abeat*) earlier *-āt.* But in accented monosyllables the long vowel remained before *-r* (*fūr, cūr*).

DIPHTHONGS

§ 131. Of the Diphthongs, *ai* and *oi* both sank to *ei,* and with orig. *ei,* further to *ī,* in unaccented syllables as in *Achīvī* (earlier *Áchaevoi) from Gr. Ἀχαιϝοί. So *olīvom,* earlier **óleivom,* earlier still *ólaevom from Gr. ἐλαῖϝον. This gives us interesting chronological data, since the *el-* must have changed to *ol-* (§ 103) before the change of *-ai-* to *-ei-* ; but *ai* must have become *ei* before the change of the accent from the first syllable in Italic to the penult (§§ 87–88).

§ 132. So in the Dat. Abl. Plur., *-īs* in the First Decl. has come from *-eis* and that from *-ais* (cf. Gr. χώραις) and in the Second Decl. from *-ois* (cf. Gr. λόγοις), Old Lat. *poploes,* becoming later *populis ;* and *-ī* in the Nom. Plur. comes from *-oi* (cf. Gr. λόγοι and Old Lat. *poploe*).

§ 133. But *ai, ae* which arose later than this change to *ei,* and later *ī,* was unaffected by it ; thus the Nom. Plur. of the 1st Declension originally ended in *-ās* (as in ͜Oscan) but was changed at some period before Plautus to *-ae* by the influence of the Pronominal ending -*ae* in such forms as *quae* (Interrogative) and *hae*, ' these (women).' These emphatic mono-syllables were accented and therefore the diphthong had remained in them unchanged all through.

§ **134.** The Diphthongs *au, ou* in unaccented syllables followed by a consonant sank to -*ū*- as in *inclūdo* beside *claudō, incūdo* from Old Lat. *caudō ' I strike, cut,' the root of which is seen in *cauda* ' the striking member, tail ' and *caussa*, later *causa* (§ **167**) from *caud-tā (§ **166**) lit. ' striking, cutting,' hence ' deciding,' hence ' case at law,' just as Gr. κρίσις ' judgement ' from κρίνω ' I separate, decide.' *caudō was super-seded by *cūdo*, taken from the compounds, just as by the time of Juvenal *claudō* had been superseded by *clūdo* taken from *in-clūdo* and the like (§ **21**).

Unaccented au, ou *before Vowels*

§ **135.** When followed by a vowel, unaccented -*au*- and -*ou*- sank to -*u*- : *dénuō* from *dē nouō* (pro-nounced as one word) ; *suus* from O. Lat. *sovos*, Gr. ἑός ' his own,' both from I.Eu. **seu̯os* (§ **112**) ; for these Pronominal Adjectives were very often Enclitic (§ **63**).

CONSONANTS

Changes of Consonant i (i̯)

§ **136.** Consonant -*i*- (-*i̯*-) was lost between vowels : *moneo* for **monei̯o*, which has the same ending as Factitive verbs like Sansk. *tarṣ-áyati* ' he makes dry,' Lat. *torreo* ' to toast,' for **tors-ei̯o*, from the same root as *terra* (see § **73** and § **190**) ; *trēs* contracted for *treies*, cf. Cretan τρέες, Attic τρεῖς, Sans. *tráyas* ' three ' (all nom. plur. masc.).

§ 137. -*mi̯*- became -*ni̯*-, and that became syllabic -*ni*-, as in *veniō* (trisyllabic) from **veni̯ō* (disyllabic) from **vemi̯ō*, I.Eu. **g͏̥mi̯ō* (§ 141).

§ 138. -*ni̯*- probably became -*nd*- as in *tendō*, Gr. τείνω from I.Eu. **ten-i̯ō*, *fendō* (§ 181), Gr. θείνω, and in the Gerundive ending -*undus*, -*endus*, probably arising in pro-ethnic Italic from -*oni̯os*, -*eni̯os* ; cf. the Sansk. Gerundive in -*an-īya-s*. On its use see § 239 (but on the Gerund see § 201).

§ 139. In Oscan and Umbrian we always have -*nn*- corresponding to Latin -*nd*-, whatever its origin, and this -*nn*- appears in words taken from these dialects, e.g. the Plautine (intentional) vulgarisms *dispennite*, *distennite*.

§ 140. -*gi̯*-, -*di̯*- became -*i̯*-, as in *māior* from **mag-i̯or* (*magnus*), *pēior* from **ped-i̯or* (*pes* ' foot,' *pedum* ' ground '), lit. ' nearer the ground, lower,' cf. the noun *pessum*, from **ped-tom* (§ 166) ' bottom,' in the old phrase *pessum ire* ' to go to the bottom, sink in ruin.'

§ 141. Otherwise -*i̯*- after a consonant became generally syllabic (-*ii̯*-) as in *capiō* (trisyllabic) beside Goth. *hafya* ' I hold,' and *venio* (§ 137).

Changes of Consonant u (u̯, *commonly written* v)

§ 142. u̯ was lost between like vowels when the first was long as in *flēram* from *flēveram*, *audīvī* which became *audiī* (§ 106), *sīs* from *sī vīs* ' if you please ' ; but not e.g. in *amāvī* nor *ăvārus*.

§ **143.** u̯ was lost before -ŏ- after a vowel, as in
deŏrsum from *dē-vorsum* (cf. § **106**) ; similarly *deus*,
oleum from *dei̯u̯os, olei̯u̯om*. Note, however, that since
the -u̯- was preserved in the Fem. *deiva*, which became
dīva, and before -ō (*deivō* later *dīvō*) we get a Re-formed
(§ **20**) Nom. and Acc. *dīvus, dīvum ;* and conversely
dea, deam.

§ **144.** -óu̯i- -óu̯e- became -ō-, as in *mōtus* from
móu̯itus, nōnus* ' ninth ' from *nóu̯enos* (§ **14), *nōram*
from *nŏveram*.

§ **145.** Hence on the pattern of *flēram, nōram*
beside *flēvi, nōvi*, arose forms like *amāram*.

§ **146.** At the end of words -u̯om and -u̯os became
-*um* and -*us* in Cicero's time, as in *boum* from earlier
bovom, ecus from earlier *equos, cum* from earlier *quom*.
But later on, in the Second Declension on the analogy
of *dominus* beside *dominī, dominō*, a new Nom. (and
Acc.) *equus* (and *equum*) were formed to match *equī,
equō*. But the form *cum* remained in all periods of
Latin after Cicero's time.

NOTE.—The spelling " *quum* " seems to have been merely
an invention of scholars in the 17th or 18th Century to distinguish
the Conjunction from the Preposition.

§ **147.** We have not enough evidence to tell precisely the conditions under which *que* and *quo* became
co as in *colō* from *quelo,—cf. Gr. τέλλομαι (§ **172**), and
inquilīnus from *en-quelēnos (§ **100** and § **129**)—and
as in *cottidiē*, from *quotitī (or *quetitī) *diē* (§ **89**) ' on
the any-numbered day, on any and every day ' ; nor
those under which *quo* became *cu*, as in *secundus* for

sequondos, an old partc. (§§ **138**, **238**) from *sequor* and so meaning ' following,' hence ' second ' or (of a wind) ' favourable,' and as in *cuius* ' of whom ' from older *quoius*. But we find *quo* preserved in the monosyllables *quod*, *quot* (and even before *m*, down to Cicero's time, § **146**), and *que* preserved in *quem* and *-que*.

Consonant u (ų) *in combination*

§ **148.** *dų-* became initially *b-* as in *bonus, bellum*, Old Latin *dųonus*, **dųellum* (though the poets finding this written form in old literary sources treated it as trisyllabic).

§ **149.** *-dų-* medially became *-ų-* as in *suāvis* for **suād-ųi-* (cf. § **246**) beside *suādeo* with the same root as in Eng. *sweet* and meaning lit. ' I make (a thing) sweet to,' hence ' I try to persuade.'

§ **150.** *pų-*, *fų-*, *bų-* lost their *u* as in *ap-erio*, *op-erio* compounds of the verb which is preserved in Lith. *-veriu* ' I open,' cf. Osc. *veru* ' gate '; and in the verbal endings *-bam*, *-bō* from *-bhų-ām*, *-bhųō* with the weak form (§§ **67** ff.) of the root seen in Gr. ὑπέρφευ ' exceedingly,' φύω ' I beget,' Lat. *fuī*. The same loss of *-ų-* appears in the words *fīō*, *du-b-ius*, *super-bus*, *vastā-bundus*, which are all derived from the same root meaning ' to be.'

§ **151.** *-sų-* between vowels (at least when the second was accented) disappeared, as in *pruīna* for **prus-ųínā*, cf. Eng. *fros-t*, Sansk. *pruṣvā* ' hoar-frost.' Contrast *Minérva* from an earlier quadrisyllable **menés-u(v)ā* (§ **186**) lit. ' Mindfulness,' cf. Gr. μένος.

§ **152.** *sųe-*, *sųo-* both became *so-* as in *soror*, acc.

soror-em from **suesōr-m̥*, Sansk. acc. *svasār-am*, I.Eu. **suesōr-m*, cf. Germ. *schwes-t-er*, Eng. *sis-t-er* (where the *-t-* was developed in pro-ethnic Germanic in some of the Cases, in which the *-r-* immediately followed the **sues-*, cf. § 79).

So Lat. *somnus* (§ 156), Sansk. *svapna-* ' sleep ' both represent directly I.Eu. **suepno- ;* a slightly different form, I.Eu. **supno-* appears in Gr. ὕπνος (for initial *s-* in Greek regularly becomes ʽ before vowels).

Lat. *sordēs* (for **suordēs*) ' soil, dirt ' contains the same root as Eng. *swart*, Germ. *schwarz* ' black.'

§ 153. In Classical Latin *-u̯-* became *-b-* only in the rare combination *-ru̯u-* (as in *ferbuī* from **fervuī*, beside *ferveo*). But in the 2nd Century A.D., Lat. *u̯* had become a Voiced Labiodental fricative like Eng. *v* (§ 43), and the Voiced Labial Plosive *b* had broken down (at least in certain positions) into the same sound ; hence consonantal *u (v)* and *b* are frequently confused then and later, as in spellings like *vene* for *bene*, *Bictorinus* for *Victorinus*.

Changes of the Plosives

§ 154. The I.Eu. Plosives (§ 54) were generally preserved in Latin, and only changed under special conditions which may now be briefly stated.

Labial Plosives

§ 155. When a word beginning with *p* had its second syllable beginning with *q*, the *p* was changed to *q* in pro-ethnic Italic : I.Eu. **peqo* ' I cook ' gave in Sanskrit *pácati* ' he cooks ' (cf. Gr. πέσσω from **peq-i̯ō*), but in Latin **quequo*, which became *coquo* (§ **147**). I.Eu. **penqe* ' five,' Sansk. *pañca*, Gr. πέντε (cf. § **172**) gave Lat. **quenque*, which became *quinque* (§ **100**).

§ **156.** Medially Lat. *p* became by assimilation

(1) *m* before *m* or *n* : *summus* for **sup-mos* (cf. *super*) ; *somnus* beside *sopor* (see further § **152**).

(2) *c* before *c* : *succurro* for **supo-curro* (for the syncope of the *-o-* in **supo* (identical with Gr. ὑπό, see § **89**).

(3) *g* before *g* : *suggero* for **supo-gero*.

(4) *b* before *d*, *i̯*, *u̯*, as in *sub-do*, *sub-iectus*, *sub-venio*.

§ **157.** From such compounds and from many phrases in which the preposition was pronounced as one word with a noun beginning with such sounds (*d*, *i̯*, *u̯*), the type *sub* came to be adopted as the regular form.

Much the same thing happened with other disyllabic prepositions ending in vowels, *ab* from **apo* (Gr. ἀπό) ; *ob* from **opi* (cf. Gr. ἐπί) ; *ad* perhaps from **ati*, Sansk. *ati* ' exceedingly,' though this Sanskrit word must also represent Gr. ἔτι ' still,' Lat. *et ;* and we must compare *ad* also with Sansk. *adhi* (§ **177**) ' towards.' But the form *at* appears in some Latin words (e.g. *atavus* ' great-great-great-grandfather ') ; as well as in the particle *at* ' but.' The Lat. *ad*, *at* therefore probably contains two I.Eu. words (cf. p. 113 footn.).

Dental Plosives

§ **158.** Initial *tl-* became *l-* as in *lātus,* older **tlātos* derived from the root seen in *tulī, tollo, tol-er-o.*

§ **159.** Before *-l-* we find *-t-* medially becoming *-c-* except after *s :* the suffix *-clum* is the same as *-τλο-* in Greek (e.g. ἐχέτλη ' handle ' from ἔχω ' I hold '), hence O. Lat. *pōclum, piāclum,* whence in Classical Latin by the 'Vowel-unfolding' regular between *-c-* and *-l-* in syllables after the accent, *pōculum, piāculum.*

Of *-stl-* we have an example in *postulāre* for **porc-stulāre* from a noun-stem **porc-stlo-,* and that from the weakest form of the root of *precor* ' I pray,' *procus* ' a wooer,' I.Eu. **prek̂-* : **prok̂-* : **pr̥k̂-* (§ **77**).

§ **160.** In composition we find the *-t* or *-d* of *at, ad* (§ **157**) assimilated

> to *p* (*appōno*)
> to *c* (*accurro*)
> to *g* (*aggero*)
> to *d* (*addo*)
> to *n* (*annuo*)
> to *l* (*alluo*)
> to *r* (*arripio*).

But it is difficult, *i.e.* our evidence is not always clear enough, for us to say whether the preposition was in the form with *-t-* or *-d-* at the time when the composition took place, and how far any particular compound was re-formed (§ **20**), so that it was actually spelt with *ad-* (e.g. *adpono*), at any particular period.

§ **161.** In any case we find *t* assimilated to *-n-*

in *annus* beside Goth. *aþn* ' year,' and *d* to *l* in *sella* ' seat ' (from *sedeo*).

§ **162.** If in words like *pandere* ' to make to open ' (beside *patēre* ' to lie open ') -*nd*- has come from -*tn*-, -*dn*-, the change must have taken place at a much earlier period, perhaps before Latin was a separate language ; *fundus* ' bottom ' beside Gr. πυθ-μήν, Eng. *bottom,* Germ. *bod-en* ' floor,' from I.Eu. *bheudh- (§ **182**), and *unda* ' wave ' beside Gr. ὕδ-ωρ, Ἁλοσ-ύδνη ' Sea-foam ' (*Iliad* 20. 207, *Odys.* 4. 404), raise the same question.

§ **163.** Final -*d* after a long vowel was lost before the time of Plautus, e.g. in the Abl. Sing. as in *praedā, meritō* from O. Lat. *praidād, meretōd.*

§ **164.** In pure Latin words I.Eu. initial and medial *d* remains, as in *dō* (Gr. δί-δω-μι ' I give '), *edo*, Sansk. *ádmi* ' I eat,' cf. Gr. ἔδομαι ' I shall eat ' (Conjunctive used as Future Indic., cf. § **280**).

§ **165.** But we find a number of words in which an original *d* has become *l*; *olēre* ' to stink ' beside *odor* ' fragrance '; *lacrima* beside Old Lat. *dacruma,*[1] Gr. δάκρυ, Eng. *tear;* *lingua* beside Eng. *tongue* (I.Eu. **dn̩gā*).

It has been recently shown that the forms with *l* were borrowed from Sabine, the change of *d* to *l* (initially and medially between vowels) being characteristic of that dialect. The particular words were adopted into Latin, each driving out the pure Latin form,

---

[1] This form was no doubt used by Ennius in the famous epitaph which he wrote for his own tomb :

> Nemo me dacrumis decoret neque funera fletu
> Faxit.—Cur ? Volito vivo(s) per ora virum.

for different reasons ; *olēre* was the form used by (Sabine) farmers to denote the smells of their own farmyards ; *lingua* was more like *lingo* ' I lick,' which comes from quite a different root (Gr. λείχω, Eng. *lick*). *lacrima* may have superseded *dacruma*, because people connected it with the adjective *lacer* ' wounded.'

§ **166.** Latin *-ss-* arose from an original *-tt-*, *-dt-*, *-dht-* (except before *-r*) as in *missus*, earlier **mit-tos*, *tōnsus*, earlier **tond-tos*, but *tōnstrīx* from **tond-trix* : also from *-ts-* or *-ds-*, as in the ending *-ōsus*, earlier *-ōs-sus* for **-od-s-os* meaning properly ' smelling of ' (as in *vīnōsus* from *vīnum* ' wine '), see § **243.**

§ **167.** After consonants and long vowels this *-ss-* became a single *-s-* some time before Cicero, who wrote double *-s-* in words like *cāssus* from *cado*, but probably only pronounced them with a single *-s-*, since the words came to be spelt with a single *-s-* directly after his time. On *caussa* for **caud-tā* from **caudo* see § **134.**

Simplification of double consonants before an accented vowel

§ **168.** Here may be noted the regular effect of the Latin Accent upon a double consonant preceding the accented vowel of the word. *-rr-*, *-ss-* and probably some other double consonants became single : as in *curúlis* from *currus*, in *disértus* ' arranging one's ideas clearly, eloquent,' an active partc. in *-tus* (§ **232**) from **dis-sértus*. So we have *o-mitto* where we should expect **ō-mitto* if it comes from **ops-mitto*. But most of the words once so affected were no doubt ' re-formed ' (§ **20**).

Velars

§ 169. Indo-European *q* was usually preserved in Latin with the labial addition of -*u̯*-, as in *sequor* : Gr. ἕπομαι : Goth. *saíhvan* : Eng. *see ;* and in *quod* : Gr. ποδ- (-απός) ' of what place ' : Eng. *what*. But in Umbrian, Oscan and Sabine I.Eu. *q* became *p*, and *lupus*, if it is the same word as Sansk. *vṛkas*, Eng. *wolf*, is probably the form used by Sabine farmers which successfully competed with a pure Lat. *luquos. On the I.Eu. Velars in Greek and Sanskrit see § 172.

§ 170. But the voiced *g̑* remained as -*gu*- only after -*n*- as in*unguo* ' I anoint ' beside Irish *imb* ' butter ' ; it appears as *g* before *r, l*, and *u* as in *gravis* : Gr. βαρύς, *glans* : Gr. βάλανος, *leg-ūmen* : Gr. λέβ-ινθος (for the Greek forms see § 172).

§ 171. Elsewhere *g̑* became *v*, as in *veniō* (see also § 200), *nūdus* from *novedos, Eng. *naked*, Gothic *naqaþs*, all descended from I.Eu. **nog̑edho-s*. Hence we must regard *bōs* (Sansk. *gaus*, Eng. *cow*) as a farmer's word borrowed from one of the country dialects (e.g. Sabine) ; the pure Latin form would have been *vūs, plural *voves, which must have sounded very much like *oves* ' sheep,'—a very undesirable confusion in the market-place ! No doubt this was one of the reasons why the farmers' pronunciation of the name was preferred to that originally current among the towns-folk of Rome.

§ 172. It is well to explain that in Greek the I.Eu. Velars appear in different forms according to the sounds

which followed them. Thus I.Eu. *q* became Gr. π
before *a*, *o*, and most consonants,

> but Gr. τ before ι, ε or ι̯
> and Gr. κ before or after *u*.

From I.Eu. *qel-* ' turn ' come Lat. *colo* ' I turn over
(the soil) ' (§ **147**), Sansk. *cárati* ' he moves ' but (1) Gr.
πόλος ' the pole-star ' (round which the heaven seems
to turn), (2) τέλλομαι ' to come round,' τέλος ' turning-
point, end,' and (3) κύκλος, ' circle,' Sansk. *cakrám*
' wheel,' a reduplicated form, almost identical with
Eng. *wheel* from *hweol*.

> So *g*   appears as β, δ and γ
>   *gh*   ,,   ,, φ, θ and χ

according to the neighbouring sounds. So in Sanskrit
from I.Eu. *q* we have *c* (pronounced as Eng. *ch*) before
i, and before *a* which represents I.Eu. *e* ; but elsewhere *k*.

Indeterminate Gutturals

§ **173.** There are a large number of words in the
Western Branches of Indo-European of which we have
not enough evidence to decide whether they originally
contained a Velar or a Palatal, or about which the
evidence is difficult to interpret. The Guttural sounds
in these words are sometimes called ' Pure Velars '
or ' Non-labialising Velars ' ; but it is perhaps best
to name them ' Indeterminate Gutturals '—using
the old name ' Guttural ' for any sound made near
the top of the throat. They will be written in what

follows simply *k* and *g*, i.e. not *q* and *g̯*, nor *k̂* and *ĝ*. For example, all that we can at present say of the Indo-European plosives from which the *c-* of Lat. *cruor* 'clotted blood' and the *-g-* of Lat. *tego* are descended is that we must call them Indeterminate Gutturals. Beside Lat. *cruor* we have Gr. κρέας 'raw flesh' and Eng. *raw* (older *hrēaw*) which point to an I.Eu. *k̂*, but Sansk. *kraviṣ* 'flesh' which points to an I.Eu. *q*. So beside *tego* we have Gr. στέγω ' I cover, conceal,' but Sans. *sthag-ayati* ' he conceals.'

It has been reasonably conjectured that these apparently irregular sounds in the different languages arose by large borrowings of words (cf. § 12) from one dialect of Indo-European into another, especially from the Western into the Eastern group, after the first separation had taken place but while the different dialects were still spoken by more or less neighbouring communities. In Latin these sounds offer no difficulty at all, since they are all treated as Palatals.

The Voiced Aspirates

§ **174.** The treatment of the Indo-European Voiced Aspirates (*bh, dh, ĝh, gh*) in Latin is one of the most marked characteristics of Latin, which separate it from all the other Italic dialects, since the Fricative sounds which represented the Indo-European Aspirates in pro-ethnic Italic, remained Fricatives medially if they remained at all in that position in Oscan and Umbrian, whereas in Latin they were generally changed into Vóiced plosives.

§ **175.** I.Eu. *bh* became initially Lat. *f-* as in *fuī* beside Greek φύω ' I beget.'

medially Lat. *-b-* as in *tibi* : Umb. *tefe*, Sans. *tubhy-(am)* ' to thee.'

§ **176.** I.Eu. *dh* : initially Lat. *f-* : *fa-c-ere*, *fē-c-ī* (§ **71**) beside Sans. *da-dhā-mi*, ' I make, put,' Gr. τί-θη-μι ' I place,' ἔ'-θηκ-α ' I placed.'

§ **177.** Medially I.Eu. *-dh-* (1) in general became *d* : I.Eu. **medhịos*, Sans. *mádhyas*, Gr. μέσσὸς, later μέσος (from **μεθịος*), Osc. *mefio-*, Lat. *medius* ' middle,' but (2) *-b-* after *u* : *iubēre* beside *iussus* (from **ịudh-tós*, § **166**) beside Sans. *yṓdhati* ' rouses to battle '; so *rubēre*, *ruber* beside *russus* ' ruddy,' cf. Osco-Lat. *rūfus* ' red-haired,' Gr. ἐ-ρεύθω ' I blush,' ἐ-ρυθρός ' red,' Sans. *rudhirás* ' red '; (3) *b* before *l* : *stabulum*, O. Lat. **stablum*, cf. Umb. *staflo-*, showing the same suffix (I.Eu. *-dhlo-*) as in Gr. γέν-εθλον ' off-spring '; (4) *b* before and after *r* : *verbum* (cf. Umb. *verfale* ' augur's platform, pulpit ') beside Eng. *word*, Lith. *vardas* ' word '; *glaber* (for **glabros*, § **183**) : Germ. *glatt* ' smooth,' Eng. *glad* (orig. of things, ' smooth, shining ') : I.Eu. **ghladhro-s*, cf. Slavonic *gladŭ-kŭ* ' smooth '; on the initial sound *gh* cf. § **173**.

§ **178.** I.Eu. *ĝh* became initially in Latin

(1) usually *h* : *hībernus*, cf. Gr. χειμερινός ' wintry,' and § **128** ;

(2) but *f* before *-u-* : *fu-ndo*, *fū-tilis* beside Gr. χυτρά ' basin, ewer,' Sans. *hutás* and Gr. χυτός, both meaning ' poured.'

(3) But in rustic and vulgar Latin initial *h-* was lost, as in the word for ' goose,' *anser* from **hans-er*,

Gr. χήν, Germ. *gans*, Eng. *goose ; arēna* from **hasēna,*
Sabine *fasēna* ' sand.'

§ 179. In Sabine, however, *ĝh-* became *f-* as in Sab.
fēdus (for the -*ē*- see § 118), pure Lat. *haedus,* Goth.
gait-ein, Eng. *goat.* So *ferrum* ' the hard metal '
is probably a word borrowed from Sabine, cf. Gr.
χερσόν ' dry land,' Marsian Latin *herna* ' stone, '
whence the tribal name *Hernici.*

§ 180. Medially *ĝh* became in Latin

(1) -*h*- between vowels : *veho* : Gr. ἔχω (older
Ϝέχω) ' I hold ' from I.Eu. *u̯eĝhō,* cf. ὄχος ' chariot,'
Eng. *way, wag-gon.*

(2) but -*g*- after a nasal : *fingo* beside Osc. *feího-*
' wall,' Gr. τεῖχος, older **θειχος,* Sans. *dēhas* ' mass '
(I.Eu. **dheiĝh-,* see below).

(3) and -*g*- before -*l*- as in *figulus* ' a potter,' earlier
*feig-los from the same root.

§ 181. I.Eu. *gh* became in Latin

(1) initially *f-* : *formus* and *furnus* ' oven,' Gr.
θερμός ' hot,' θέρος ' summer,' cf. Ligurian *Bormio*
a place with hot springs, *Bormanus* a god of hot springs ;
fendō : Gr. θείνω 'I strike,' φόνος ' murder ' (§§ 172, 138).

(2) medially -*v*-, -*gu*- or -*g*- just as I.Eu. *g* : *ninguere,*
nivem, nix (for **nigs*) beside Gr. νίφα (acc.) ' snow ' ;
frāgrāre beside Gr. ὀσ-φρα-ίνομαι (ὀσ- for **ods-,* cf.
Lat. *odor*), a reduplicated verb from a root **ghrā-*
' to smell.'

Roots with two Aspirates

§ 182. The student should note that many I.Eu.
roots contained two Aspirates, but that one of these,

in consequence of different Phonetic changes, regularly became a Plosive in Sanskrit and in Greek. Thus from an I.Eu. stem *bhudhen- (Germ. boden, Eng. bottom) came Lat. fund- in fundus (see § 162) but Sans. budhna- and Gr. πυθ- in πυθ-μήν—all with the same meaning. So Lat. fīdo is identical with Gr. πείθω ' I persuade,' I.Eu. *bheidhō ' I trust ' and ' I make to trust.'

§ 183. The Indeterminate Gutturals (see § 173) were in general treated in Latin as if they were Palatals ; examples of Aspirates of this category appear in hostis, I.Eu. *ghos-ti-s, Slav. gostĭ, Germ. gast, Eng. guest, and in glaber (see § 177 (4)).

Peculiar features in Borrowed Words

§ 184. In words which were borrowed into Latin by one or another popular channel, e.g. through the language of sailors and traders, ultimately from Greek, but which may have come through some other dialect (Oscan, Messapian, or Etruscan) on their way, we find certain peculiar changes.

Voiced and Breathed sounds are frequently confused, as in Lat. gubernare ' to steer,' Gr. κυβερνᾶν, Lat. taeda (nom.) from Gr. δᾳς, acc. δᾳδα ' a torch.'

The Greek Breathed Aspirates (§ 50) often appear with their Plosive part doubled, Lat. bracchium (with a long first syllable) from Gr. βραχίων ' fore-arm,' Lat. struppus from Gr. στρόφος ' twist, turn ' ; Vulgar Latin *muttus (cf. § 111), whence Ital. motto, Fr. mot, from Greek μῦθος ' a story.'

§ **185.** I.Eu. *s* was preserved in Latin initially before vowels (e.g. *sēmen*, beside Eng. *sow, seed*) and Breathed Plosives (as in *sterno* beside Eng. *strow*), and finally ; medially also before Breathed Plosives (as in *est*, Gr. ἐστί ' is '). But it suffered many changes under other conditions.

§ **186.** Between vowels *s* became *r* between 450 and 350 B.C. : *āra* from older *āsa ;* in the oblique Cases of nouns like *genus*, e.g. *generis*, older **geneses* (§§ **121, 122**), cf. Gr. γένους, older γένεος (from **γενεσος); Sans. *jánasas* ' of a race.' The ordinary Infinitive in *-ere* is the Locative of a Verbal noun formed with this Suffix, see further §§ **243, 278**.

§ **187.** So in the Verb *es-se* ' to be ' (§ **278**) beside *est, estis* of the Present we have *eram, ero*. An old Inf. **erom*, Osc. *esom* ' to be,' seems [1] to be added to the Dat. (or Loc.) of the Verbal Noun in *-tu-*, of which the ' Supines ' are the Acc. and Loc. respectively, to form in Old Lat. a Fut. Inf. in *-ūrum ;* this was to start with invariable whatever its Subject, as in a sentence quoted by Gellius, *scio inimicos meos hoc dicturum* ' I know that my enemies will say this.' Later on the form in *-ūrum* was regarded as agreeing with any Masc. Acc. which was used as its Subject, and hence inflected to agree with a Fem. or Plur. subject, and so the so-called Future Partc. in *-ūrus* was created. But in Plautus the Inf. is used without *esse* in four-fifths of its occurrences ; and Cicero prefers to omit it ; these are traces of the older use.

[1] See further, p. 126.

Words with intervocal -s-

§ 188. But a considerable number of words came into Latin partly from neighbouring dialects, with -*s*- between vowels, after 350 B.C., when the change had ceased. Hence these words show -*s*-, as *cāseus* ' cheese,' *rosa* probably from S. Oscan *rodia*, (cf. Gr. ῥόδον ' rose,' ῥοδέα ' rosebush ') with -*s*-, sounded -*z*- from -*di̯*- just as -*s*- from -*ti̯*- in Osc. *Bansa*-, Lat. *Bantia* ; *miser* a term of abuse (such terms are often borrowed) beside Gr. μυσαρός (probably with its irregular -*s*- between vowels also borrowed from some dialect of South Italy) and many more. Again, in the participles in -*sus* (like *fūsus*), the -*ss*- had not become -*s*- at the time of the change of -*s*- to -*r*- (§§ **166–7**).

s *in combination*

§ 189. *sr*- became *þr* (with the sound of Eng. *thr*- in *throw*) in pro-ethnic Italic and this became initially *fr*- as in *frīgus* : Gr. ῥῖγος (I.Eu. **srīgos*), but medially -*br*- as in *fūnebris* ' funereal ' from *fūnus* (stem *fūnes*-) ' funeral rite.'

§ 190. Medial -*rs*-, -*ls*- became -*rr*-, -*ll*-, as in *ferre, velle* for **fer-se, *vel-se* (cf. *es-se*), *olle, ille* probably for **ol-so, *il-so* (§ **105**), where **so* is identical with Gr. ό, Sans. *sa* ' he.' *ācerrimus, facillimus* from **ācer-somo-s, *facil-somo-s* (§ **255**). At the end of words the -*rr*- became simply -*r*-, as in *ter* (§ **128**), *puer* from **puerr*, older **puers*, older still **pueros*.

§ 191. Before *m, n, l,* or *v*, medial -*s*- vanished, having previously caused the loss of any preceding

Plosive or -*n*- ; and the preceding vowel, if short, was lengthened as in *prīmus* from **prismos*, N. Oscan *prismu* ' prima ' beside Lat. *pris-cus*. *rēmus* (cf. Old Lat. *tri-resmos*) for **ret-s-mos*, cf. Gr. ἐ-ρετ-μός ' oar.'

iūmentum ' yoked-cattle, beasts of burden,' from Old Lat. *iouxmentum* older **i̯eu̯gs-mentom*, cf. Gr. ζύγον, Lat. *iugum, iungo* ; *i̯eu̯g-s-* is the weakest form of the noun stem which appears in Gr. ζεῦγ-ος ; *rāmentum* for **rād-s-mentum* from *rādō*.

lūna from **leu̯csnā*, Praenestine *losna*, Zend. *raoχsna*, cf. Gr. λευκός ' white,' Lat. *lūceō*.

tēlum ' dart,' from **tens-lom* or **tends-lom* (lit. ' weapon of aiming ') ; *trānāre* from **trans-nāre*.

sēvirī from **sex-virī*, *ēvellō* from **ex-vellō*, *ē-mittō* from **ex-mittō*, and so *ē-līdo*, *ē-numerō* and the like ; from such forms arose the preposition *ē* beside *ex*.

§ **192.** *Similarly* -*sd*- became -*d*-, as in *īdem* (masc.) from **is-dem*; and -*rsd*- became -*rd*- as in *hordeum* ' barley ' for **horzdeom* closely akin to Germ. *Gerste*.

NOTE.—The formation of the pronoun *īdem* is typical of the way in which pronouns grow up. The neut. *id-em* is simply *id*, whose ending is identical (§ **60** (4)) with the *t* of Eng. *it*, extended by the particle of emphasis -*em* which appears also in Sans. *id-am* ' that.' Then -*dem* came to be felt to be characteristic of the word and was applied bodily to the masc. and fem. forms, driving out **is-em* (if it ever existed in Latin).

§ **193.** Before *n*-, *m*-, *l*-, or *f*-, initial *s*- disappeared, as in *nūbo* ' I veil myself, marry ' (of the bride) beside Slav. *snubiti* ' to love, pay court to ' (hence *cōnūbium* for **com-snūbium*, cf. § **191**) ; *mīror* beside Sansk.

smáyate ' he laughs,' Eng. *smi-le ;* *lūb-ricus* beside
Goth. *sliupan,* Eng. *slip ; fungus* beside or borrowed
from Gr. σφόγγος. Compare *dif-fero* from **dis-fero.*

Consonant r *and Consonant* l

§ **194.** Medial *-r-* was lost before *-s-* which had
come from *-ss-,* as in *prōsus, prōsa ōrātiō* ' speech going
straight on, not stopped at the end of a line, prose ' ;
and before *-s-* followed by a Breathed Plosive, as in
tōstus for **torstus* from *torreo* (for **torseo,* § **190,** cf.
Gr. τερσ-αίνω ' I make dry ') ; *posco* for **porc-sco*
(§§ **197** and **159**).

§ **195.** In suffix-syllables *-l-* became *-r-* if the word
contained *l* in any previous syllable. Thus from the
suffix *-clum* (§ **159**) we get *-crum* in *lavā-crum* ' washing-
basin ' ; from the suffix *-li-* we get *-ri-* in *mīlitāris,*
ālāris as well as in Neut. nouns like *calca-r* (contrast
anima-l) ; in these cases final *-e* (from earlier *-i,* § **99** (1))
has been lost.

§ **196.** *-ln-* and *-nl-,* and also *-rl-,* became *-ll-* as in
collis for **col-nis,* cf. Gr. κολωνός ' hillock,' Lith.
kálnas ' hill ' ; *homullus, gemellus* from **homon-lo-s,*
*gemen-lo-s (cf. *homo, gemini*) ; *agellus* from **ager-lo-s*
from **agro-lo-s* (§ **128**).

Sonant r *and Sonant* l (ŗ *and* ļ)

§ **197.** I.Eu. ŗ became *-or-* in Latin as in *fors,*
Sans. *bhṛtís* ' a bringing, arriving, chance,' which contained the Weak form (§ **70**) of the root of *fero.* So
in *cornum,* Gr. κράνον ' cornel cherry ' ; *porrum* for

*porsom (§ **190**), Gr. πράσον 'leek'; posco from *porc-scō (§ **194**), I.Eu. pr̥k̑-sk̑ō, containing the weakest form (§ **77**) of the root of precor ' I pray.'

§ **198.** I.Eu. l̥ became -ol- and that generally (§ **104** (2)) -ul- as in multa ' fine,' Old Lat. molta, for *molcta, cf. mulcāre ' to chastise,' Sans. marcáyati ' he injures,' cf. Gr. βλαβή from *μλαβά and that from I.Eu. *ml̥g-ā(§ **172**).

Nasals

§ **199.** Final -m in Latin was weakly sounded, hardly more than as a nasal colour (§ **47**) to the vowel, which, however, made the syllable long. Hence a syllable ending in -m was freely elided in poetry, just as if it ended in a vowel.

§ **200.** Medial -m- became -n- before i̯ as in venio earlier *veni̯o from *vemi̯o (§ **171**) ; and before t and d and s as in con-tendo, con-do, con-sero and the like, all from com- ' with, together ' ; quando from *quam-do ' at what point ' (see § **201**). But ēmptus from emo, cōmpsi from cōmo are Re-formates made after the changes of -m-s- to -n-s-, -m-t- to -n-t- was over, and showing a different treatment of the re-formed combination at the later date.

§ **201.** Notice especially the origin of the Verbals in -undo, -endo which contain the post-position -dō ' to, at ' (identical (§ **60** (4)) with Eng. to, Germ. zu) and the acc. of the verbal root-noun which we have seen in the old Oscan Inf. esom (§ **187**).

This probably had two forms—one in -om (Thematic, § **274**), and one in -em (Non-thematic, § **277**) ; that in -*em* corresponds to what became the Pass. Inf. (*ag-ī, reg-ī*) which was properly a Dative of the same Verbal noun ' for doing,' ' for ruling.' Thus *agun-do agen-do* meant properly ' towards doing ' or ' in doing.' But it looked like a Dat. or Abl., and so arose the so-called Gerund, used either in the -*ndo* form alone regarded as a kind of half-wild Ablative, or in this same Ablative with the preposition *in*, or in the newly formed Acc. in -*ndum* with *ad* or *in*, but very rarely with any other prepositions.

This became associated with the old partc. in -*ndus* through the resemblance of the two forms. This partc. had a different origin (§ **138**) but its use was curiously limited by the new association with the ' Gerund,' see § **239**.

§ **202.** Initially *mr-* became *fr-*, but medially -*br-* as in *fraces* ' lees of wine,' beside *marcidus* ' rancid.'

hībernus from *heim-ri-nos (§§ **128**, **178**), cf. Gr. χειμερινός ' wintry,' from the I.Eu. disyllabic root **g̑heiem-* appearing in Latin in two different weakenings (§ **69**), *g̑heim-* as in this word, and **g̑hi-em-* (*hiems*). So *tuber* ' swollen root ' for *tub-ro-s (§ **128**) and that for *tum-ro-s from the root which appears in *tum-idus* ' swollen.'

Sonant m *and* n (m̥ *and* n̥)

§ **203.** I.Eu. m̥ and n̥ became *em, en* in Latin and were treated just like original *em* and *en* : e.g. in Accusatives like *pedem*, cf. Gr. Acc. πόδα, ' foot ' (§ **70**).

So Lat. *decem*, Gr. δέκα, Sans. *dáça; tentus* (§ **69**), Gr. τατός, Sansk. *tatás*.

VII. HOW LATIN GRAMMAR WAS BUILT UP

A. THE SHAPING OF NOUNS, ADJECTIVES AND ADVERBS

§ **204.** Most of the changes we have so far considered are Phonetic ; that is, they were all unconscious, and happened before the speakers who made them knew that they had made any change at all. Now we can take a step further and apply this knowledge of the Phonetic Laws of Latin to a study which directly contributes to our understanding the use of the language and the thought of the authors who wrote in it ; that is, to studying the changes and developments of Grammar made consciously by some speakers of the language and adopted more or less deliberately by all. This part of the subject is called Morphology, by which we mean the history of the grammatical forms, Declensions, Conjugations and the like. This cannot be studied profitably in its details without a wide knowledge of many kindred languages, and no complete account of Latin Morphology will be here attempted. But it will be useful to consider a certain number of conspicuous innovations which come under our notice

frequently in considering the derivation of particular
words, and which are themselves among the most
characteristic features of Latin. As we proceed, we
shall become acquainted with the suffixes which were
most commonly used in Latin to form Nouns, Adjectives,
Adverbs, and Verbs.

Gender

§ **205.** By the G e n d e r of a noun we mean the
answer to the question whether, when an adjective
is attached to it, that adjective is to stand in what
we call the masc., fem., or neut. form ; and similarly,
when the place of the noun is taken by a pronoun,
whether the form of that pronoun is to be masc., fem.,
or neut.

§ **206.** In modern English there is no Gender at all,
except in some pronouns such as *he, she, it,* one of which
we choose according as we regard the noun for which
it stands as representing a male or female person or
merely a thing. So far therefore as there is any
Gender in modern English, its forms express two
definite meanings, the idea of living personality and the
idea of sex. It is true, however, that we sometimes
personify non-living things like a ship or an engine,
a city or a church, and speak of them as if they were
female creatures. But in other languages no such
personification is implied by the use of the masc. or
fem. endings in Nouns or Adjectives. French people
do not think of *le ciel* (' the sky ') as a man because it
is masculine nor of *la douleur* (' pain ') as a woman
because it is feminine. Nor did the Romans attribute

male sex to *lembus* ' a rowing-boat ' or female sex
to *navis* ' a ship,' or think of either as more endowed
with life than *navigium* (neut.) which is the general
name for ' vessel ' of any kind or size.

§ **207.** This absence of Gender in modern English
creates special difficulty for English students in learning
any other language. It is true that fem. forms in Latin
and other Indo-European languages do sometimes
denote female sex, and that the neut. forms do nearly
always denote something which is not living, but this
was not the original meaning of the endings, and they
have only been forced into denoting it in a limited
number of words and forms.

§ **208.** The only common difference between masc.
and fem. endings on the one hand and neut. endings
on the other, in any Indo-European language, is the
use of the neut. -*m* to distinguish the acc. from the nom.
case in masc. and fem. words, and so to show whether
the speaker regards a particular word as denoting the
subject or the object of the action. This was quite
a splendid feat of grammatical invention, but it took
place at such a very early period of the parent I.Eu.
language that nothing more can be usefully said about
it here ; though we may note that it was lost again
when different bodies of barbarians cut down Latin
into the different Romance languages ; and that
our own language was robbed of the power of expressing
this distinction (save in Pronouns like *thee, him,
them*) when English came to be spoken by the Normans.

The Feminine Endings

§ **209.** But we know more about the original meaning of the endings which we find partly used to denote female sex, especially the -*a* in nouns, pronouns and adjectives.

All the nouns of what we call the First Declension as well as the nom. and acc. pl. neut. of the Second Declension, which had originally the same ending, denoted to start with a C o l l e c t i o n of things or persons, and hence the general character which they shared or the process of collecting them. This we express in grammar by saying that the -*ā*- Suffix marked Collective or Abstract nouns.

§ **210.** This appears plainly in Latin words like *repulsa* ' defeat ' beside the partc. *repulsus* ' defeated,' and also in a few old forms like *loca*. Beside the singular *locus* ' a place,' we have not merely the ordinary plur. *loci* ' (particular) places,' but in the nom. and acc. the old form *loca* ' a set of places, a district ' ; and in poetry we have a great many neut. pl. words used in this way ; e.g. from *tectum* ' a covered place, roof ' we have *tecta* which often means ' a set of covered rooms ' i.e. ' a house ' ; *arma* ' a set of weapons ' i.e. a man's armour. Similarly *pro-fugus* means ' a man who runs away ' ; but the fem. noun *fuga* means ' people running away, flight.' And it is true to say that in all feminine nouns in Greek and Latin, except those which have been definitely tied down to denote female sex, we find some such Collective or Abstract meaning ; so that, in general, all Abstract Nouns, with whatever suffix they were formed (with -*ā*- or

-ti- or *-īe-* or *-tiōn-*), had properly feminine Gender. This Gender is often very important as showing the original character of many words which were to start with Collective or Abstract, but later were tied down to a concrete meaning (§ 215).

§ 211. It is worth while to note in passing that this is why neuter plural words in Greek, when they are subject to a verb, have that verb in the singular. The neut. plur. ending had at an earlier stage marked a Collective noun.

The use to denote sex

§ 212. But how did it come about that a suffix with this abstract meaning should have been applied to denote female sex ? It has been shown recently that this new meaning arose in two ways : (1) because certain very old forms, which existed long before there was any such thing as gender, happened to end in the same sounds as one or other of the suffixes which later on came to be used to make Collective nouns ; especially the very ancient feminine pronoun *sā* ' she ' which occurs in Sanskrit, and appears in Greek as *ἡ* (Doric *ἁ*).

(2) because a number of Collective nouns which corresponded to masculine nouns denoting animals and which properly meant the ' herd ' or ' pack ' of the particular animals, came to be applied to distinguish the family as distinguished from its male head. For example, the word *lupus* or rather the I.Eu. word from which it is descended (see § 169), meant ' the wolf,' especially the male wolf who hunted for prey with whom shepherds and others were unpleasantly

G

familiar ; contrasted with this, other forms (*vṛkī* in Sanskrit, *lupa* in farmer's Latin (§ **169**), λύκαινα in Greek) originally meant ' the wolfery,' that is, the various female wolves and their cubs who depended on the male ; so *equos* meant originally ' the male horse, stallion,' *equa* originally ' the herd of mares and foals.' Then the feminine form came later on to be applied especially to one particular mate. The English word *hen* and its German equivalent *Henne* (fem.) properly meant ' the hennery, the fowls '; whereas the masculine form (Germ. *Hahn,* lost in English) meant ' the cock.'

§ **213.** These forms are quoted from the separate languages, but of course the new meaning had been developed long before either Latin or Greek or Sanskrit or Germanic was divided from the parent speech ; thus at the very earliest period of Latin *equa* had already the meaning ' mare '; at the very earliest period of German *Henne* had the meaning ' hen.'

§ **214.** The different types of meaning developed from the Collective sense may be prettily illustrated by the suffix -*īna*. In words like *farīna* ' corn-meal, corn,' it is Collective ; in *ruīna* ' the process of falling,' *rapīna* ' robbery,' *medicīna* ' treatment,' it is generally Abstract, but sometimes Collective, ' ruins,' ' booty,' ' medicine.' In *tonstrīna* ' a barber's shop,' *fodīna* ' a mine,' it denotes the place where the operations are carried on. But the other use of the suffix, to denote female creatures, had been established before Latin was a separate language, as in *rēgīna* from *rēx, gallīna* ' hen ' from *gallus* ' cock.'

§ **215.** Some of these words show the character-istic Latin tendency to restrict the meaning of an abstract term, or, as we say, to ' narrow it down,' so that it shall denote merely some concrete thing. So *toga*, properly ' the act of covering,' meant in Latin simply a particular garment; *cauda*, properly 'striking,' came to mean simply the striking member of an animal, ' the tail '; *scrība*, properly, ' writing, clerkage,' merely ' a clerk,' and its gender was then changed to be masculine. So the suffix *-tā*, originally Collective or Abstract in words like *iuventa* ' youth,' *senecta* ' old age,' came in words like *nauta* to mean not ' the ship's complement, the crew,' but simply ' a sailor.' Words of this type were marked as masculine in Greek by a change in their declension ; instead of **naȩtā* the nom. was made ναύτης (Dor. ναύτᾱς), and a new gen. ναύτου was invented, beside the old acc. ναύτην (Dor. ναύτᾱν) ; in Latin the words suffered no change in form, but only in gender.

§ **216.** This process of ' concretising ' affected a large class of nouns in Latin formed with the suffix *-ti-* which properly denoted a verbal action. *vestis*, properly ' clothing,' came to mean ' garment, cloth,' though it always retained something of a Collective meaning. *postis*, properly ' a placing,' came to mean ' door-post '; *vectis*, properly ' a lifting, a carrying,' came to mean ' a beam, lever '; and these two words became masculine (§ **219**) ; *ratis*, properly ' a contriv-ing ' (from *reor, ratus*), came to mean ' a contrivance for floating, a raft ' (§ **219**) ; just as, conversely, from Gr. σχεδία 'raft' was formed the verb σχεδιάζειν ' to act or speak in haste, improvise.' The result was that the suffix -ti- was no longer felt to express verbal action properly, and it was replaced by a combination of itself with an additional suffix -ōn-. So the new word ratiō 'thinking, reasoning' took the place of ratis in this sense. This compound suffix had been created before Latin was a separate language, since it appears in several kindred languages, but it was applied very widely in Latin. Indeed it is still a 'living' suffix, that is, new words are continually being formed by it in Romance languages and in English (e.g. electrification, nationalisation).

§ 217. A common method by which an abstract noun is restricted to a concrete meaning is by putting it in the plural; e.g. for the concrete meaning 'a ruin' we have generally the plural ruinae. Similarly copia means 'abundance,' copiae 'resources' or 'military forces'; and hence many words were never used in the singular like insidiae, 'troops in ambush' or 'place of ambush.'

Masculine names in -a in Latin

§ 218. Probably the only nouns of the First Declension in Latin in which no original abstract meaning can be found are a small group of masc. names like Porsenna, Cinna, Sulla, Catilina, Perperna. All these have recently been shown to be of Etruscan origin and so not strictly Latin at all. The facts recorded about these particular persons show that they had their full share of the cruelty which seems to have been characteristic of the Etruscans (see, for instance, Vergil's account of the Etruscan king Mezentius, *Aen.* viii. 481–8—a story well worthy of the Etruscan's modern rival, the Turk).

Change of Gender

§ **219.** Gender is frequently modified by Analogy, since words of similar meaning tend to take the same gender. Thus *arbōs, arboris* may itself have owed its fem. gender to some word of similar meaning in the First Declension, or may have been always feminine, meaning something like ' growth ' ; but in either case it pushed its Gender upon all the names of trees of whatever declension (*ornus, fāgus,* and the rest). So probably it was the word *fluvius* that gave the masculine gender generally to names of rivers (*Tiberis, Anio*) and to the word *amnis.* Some of the words in *-tis* which have taken a particularly concrete meaning like *postis, vectis* became masculine, on the pattern perhaps of some other word with concrete meaning like *stipes, lapis, murus ;* but *ratis* was probably kept feminine because that was the gender of *nāvis.*

§ **220.** It is worth while to add that the abstract meaning of the feminine gender clearly survives in the Romance languages. Thus in French, nouns in *-eur* like *pudeur* ' modesty,' *honneur* ' honour,' have taken this gender from words like *gloire,* ' glory,' *vertu* ' virtue,' though they are derived from words which in Latin are masculine (*pudor, honor*).

Formative Elements in Nouns and Adjectives

§ 221. To derive any word we have always to analyse it, at least as far as we can, into its different elements, by comparing it with kindred words. In an English group of words, for instance, such as *man, man's, man-hood, man-ly, man-li-est, un-man-n-ed,* we can generally recognise some common and most essential element, here the syllable *man ;* all the other elements are called F o r m a n t s though they are of different kinds, *un-* a P r e f i x, *-'s, -hood,* and the rest various S u f f i x e s. When we find one common element in a number of words in different Indo-European languages, we call that element the I.Eu. R o o t, though often we cannot tell whether it ever existed as a word by itself without any Formants.

§ 222. The student is already familiar with the endings that mark different Numbers and Cases in Nouns and Adjectives, and different Numbers and Persons in Verbs. But it will be useful to give here, in the simplest form, a list of the chief Suffixes that were in use in Latin, forming either what we call the Stems of Nouns and Adjectives, or the Stems of the different Tenses in Verbs, and to indicate briefly the particular meaning or meanings which any of them expressed in Latin.

The meaning of one set of Suffixes, those connected with Gender, has already been discussed.

Noun and Adjective Stems

§ 223. Sometimes we find the Case-endings directly following the Root, which itself acts as a Stem, as in *rēx* (from *rēg-s), *rēg-is ; re-dux, re-duc-is* ' returning, safely restored.' All this class are called R o o t - N o u n s.

§ 224. From a verbal Root-Noun was formed the Passive Infinitive, so far as it was originally a Dative ; e.g. *ag-ī* ' for action, for doing, for being done ' (cf. **§§ 187, 201**). But the same form would be also the Locative (from earlier *-ei*) of the Thematic Stem (**§ 274** f.) of the Verb, when that stem was used as a Noun ; in that case the meaning was ' in acting, in ruling.'

On the forms in *-ier* see **§ 316.**

§ 225. The two forms in *-m* which, as we have seen, underlie the Gerund in *-dō* (**§ 201**) are respectively the Accus. of the Root-Noun from Non-Thematic (**§ 277**) Tenses, e.g. *ferem in *ferendō,* and from Thematic Tenses (**§ 274**), e.g. *regom in *regundō.* Afterwards the *-endō* form was extended to all verbs alike and the *-undō* forms were ' levelled out,' though we find them in early poetry and old legal formulae, e.g. *feriundo* ' for striking,' *i.e.* coining, in the title of the commissioners of the Roman mint (**§ 239**, NOTE).

NOTE.—The old Infinitive *esom later *erom* meaning ' to be ' (**§ 187**) must be ranged as a Thematic form beside the " Future " *ero*, **§ 280.**

§ 226. The commonest class of Suffixes are those which make the First and Second Declensions, whose stems are said to end in *-ā-* and *-o-* because these sounds underlie nearly all the different forms. This we could not tell from Ciceronian Latin alone, where, for instance, the endings -os and -om in Nom. and Acc. Sing. Masc. have become -us and -um (§ 127), though we find them in Early Latin and in Greek. It is convenient to enumerate the Masc. Neut. and Fem. types together, though in Nouns the Feminine form of any Suffix generally has a different meaning from the Masc. or Neut. (see e.g. § 209).

Strictly we should speak not of -o- stems but of " -e- : -o- stems " because in the Vocative (domine, cf. Gr. ἄδελφε ' oh brother ') and Locative (humī, older humei, ' on the ground,' cf. Gr. οἴκει ' at home ') the stem appears in the form -e-, which stands in some relation of Ablaut (§ 73) to the -o- of the other cases. But for simplicity's sake we call this common class of nouns " the -o- stems."

§ 227. Chief of these are :

-o-, -ā- : Nouns, as lūc-us, tog-a, sol-um ; Adjectives, as bon-us.

-io-, -iā- ; -vo-, -vā- ; -ro-, -rā- ; -lo-, lā- ; -mo-, -mā- ; -no-, -nā- ; -co-, -cā- ; to-, -tā- ; -so-, -sā- (§ 262) ; -do-, -dā- (from I.Eu. -dho, -dhā, as in lūci-dus, acer-bus, see § 177).

§ 228. From these were derived others such as -ello-, -tīvo-, -āno- ; -īno- ; -mento- (Neut.) ; -ndo- ; -tīnā-, -trīnā-. Examples of these used in special meanings will be found below.

§ 229. Other Vowel-Suffixes are

-i- as in ov-i-s, also -ti- (§ 216) and in a few words -mi-, -ni- and (mostly in Adjectives) -ri-, -li-. -vi- ;

-u- as in *grad-u-s* (gen. *grad-ūs*) and a large class of
Verbal Nouns in *-tu-* (like *sta-tu-s*) parallel to the
Participles in *-to-*. From these *-tu-* Nouns are derived,
the so-called ' Supines,' the Acc. in *-tum* used to denote
the purpose of some journey or commission, the Abl.
in *-tū* being used with a few adjectives which describe
the character of an action, as in e.g. *horrendum dictū*
' horrible in the telling,' *difficile factū* ' hard to do.'

§ **230.** Thus from Verbs of the *-ā-* Conjugation came
Abstract Nouns in *-ātu-* as *dominātus* ' mastering,
mastery, domination.' On the analogy of such words
(*dominātus* beside *dominārī*, and beside *dominus*)
arose others where there was no Verb, but only a Noun,
e.g. *principātus* ' holding the first place ' from *princeps*
' first man.' Hence *-ātu-* came to be felt as a suffix
denoting public office, as in *magistrātus* : *magister,
cōnsulātus* : *cōnsul.*

§ **231.** The suffix *-iē-*, as in *fac-iē-s*, had by Ablaut
(§ **71**) also the form *-ia-* (*māteriēs* and *māteria*) ; its
weakest form was *-ī-* to which in Latin a further suffix
-c- was added as in *da-tr-ī-c-* beside *datōr-* (see below).

Participles

§ **232.** The suffix *-to-* was originally Adjectival, meaning ' affected by, full of,' as in Lat. *ānsā-tus, sceles-tus.*
Then it was attached to Verbs, both with A c t i v e
meaning (as in *tacitus, disertus* and all Deponents) ;
but later, i.e. as a living suffix in Ciceronian Latin, it had
regularly P a s s i v e meaning (*amātus*). See further
p. 126.

§ **233.** This Participle was also originally T i m e -

l e s s, and this meaning survives in many forms, e.g. *ratus* 'thinking,' *citus*, 'moving swiftly,' and very often in poetry (e.g. *cantu solata laborem* 'relieving her toil by singing,' Vergil, *Georg.*, i. 293).

§ 234. The other chief Participial ending was the Active -*(e)nt*-, which in -*iens*, -*euntis* shows the old Ablaut-variation (§ 70), but has elsewhere been 'levelled' by Analogy to contain always the vowels of the Verb-stem, -*ant*-, -*ent*-, -*ient*-.

§ 235. On the Future Participle in -*tūro*- see § 187.

The Gerundive and other forms in -ndo-

§ 236. On the origin of the Gerundive in -*ndo*-, meaning 'fit to be (done),' 'likely to be (done),' see § 138.

§ 237. But this ending -*ndo*- came into Latin also with the meaning of a Present Participle, Passive and Intrans., as we see in old phrases like *volvenda dies* 'rolling time'; and in the forms in -*bundus*, which is really a Partc. from the root of *fuī* (for the -*b*- see § 175) meaning 'being,' attached to the Stem of the Present (§ 284) used as a Locative Case, *vastā-bundus*, lit. 'being in (the act of) laying waste.'

A few forms in -*cundus*, like *fācundus* 'eloquent' (*fārī* 'to speak'), seem to be made on the pattern of *fēc-undus* which is from the Normal Form (§ 71) of the root of *facio* and so means 'making, creative, fertile.'

§ 238. If the suffix comes from -*en-i̯o*-, -*on-i̯o*- (as suggested in § 138) its original meaning would be merely 'connected with' the action of the Verb, and in some Verbs, especially transitive Verbs, this might develop the notion of 'fit to be,' 'bound to be' (e.g. **bher-*

enįo-, Lat. *ferendo-* ' bound to be borne ') ; but in others, especially intransitive Verbs, merely that of a Present Partc. (e.g. *rotundo-* ' connected with rolling, rolling, round,' *-bundo-* ' connected with being, being ').

It is important to notice that whether the derivation from *-en-įo-* is correct or not (and much the same meaning would arise if the last syllable were identical with the *-do-*, of adjj. like *lucidus*, which comes from *-dho-*, see § **177**), there is no doubt whatever about the Participial and Intransitive side of the use of this group of forms.

§ **239.** But how did the Gerundive from being a Present Partc. and a Passive Verbal of Expected Action come to be used, in agreement with the noun which was the object of the Verbal action, to describe that action itself, as in the familiar but very curious idiom of which *ad pacem petendam*, and *pacis petendae causa* are the common types ?

The answer lies in the accidental resemblance between this old participle in *-ndo-* and the ' Gerund,' whose development from a post-positional phrase we have traced in § **201**.

Since in early Latin on the one hand

    (a) *petendō pācem* ' for (or ' in ') seeking peace ' ;
    (b) *petendī pācem* ' of seeking peace ' ;
    (c) *ad petendum pācem* ' towards seeking peace ' :
    (d) *agrōs dōnandī causā* ' for the sake of giving land ' ;

and on the other hand

    (e) *pāx petenda* ' the peace that is to be sought '
    (f) *agrī dōnandī* ' the lands that should be given,'

were all established phrases, and since, further, the meaning of (c) and (d) could be also more simply expressed, to some extent, by *ad pācem* and *agrōrum causā* respectively, it seemed natural to change (c) into *ad p e t e n d a m pācem* and sometimes (d) into *agrōrum dōnandōrum causā*, though the type (d) had not gone out of use, as (c) had, by the time of Cicero.

That this is a true account of what happened may be said to be proved by the i n t e r m e d i a t e type of phrase which is sometimes found, as in Lucretius', *poenārum soluendī tempus*, which is literally ' the time of penalties, of paying (them) ' ; this shows clearly the connexion which was felt between the word, here *tempus*, which governed the Gerund and the noun which denoted the object of the action which the Gerund described.

The result was to force upon the old Passive or Intransitive Participle, which to start with described Action-present or Action-to-be-expected, a new use which in meaning was equivalent to a phrase in which the active Gerund governed an object in the accusative.

NOTE.—This dependence on the Gerund explains some other curious features in the use of the Gerundive forms, for instance, the fact that, like the Gerund, they are rarely if ever used after any Prepositions but those akin in meaning to the Post-position *-dō* (*in*, *ad*, *super*, *inter*) ; and the curious uncertainty as to the Case of many phrases ; e.g. in Vergil's *labor curandis vitibus*, have we a " Dative of Work Contemplated " or an Ablative of the ' region within which ' ? The truth is, we have neither, but only a reflexion of the use of the Post-position *-dō* which gave *curandō* the meaning ' in (and ' for ') tending.' The

Romans themselves hesitated ; in the title of the Commissioners of the Mint (which according to numismatists is not earlier than the last Century B.C.), *tresviri auro argento aere flando feriundo* ' commissioners, numbering three, for smelting and stamping gold and silver and bronze,' *aere* cannot be called a Dative, nor indeed anything but an Ablative.

Participial -meno-

§ **240.** The Participial suffix *-meno-* which is so common in Greek has almost disappeared in Latin, save in a few old words which show the weaker (§ **69**) form *-mno-*, e.g. *alumnus* ' foster-child ' from *alo* ' I nourish, rear.'

§ **241.** But the Masc. and Fem. Nom. Plur. of the old Partc. in *-o-meno-s*, which by phonetic changes (§§ **122, 131**–2) had both come to end in *-iminī*, had been used with parts of the Verb ' to be ' (though this was often omitted) to form a kind of Passive ; *e.g.* such phrases as *regiminī sumus, estis, sunt,* were once used to mean ' we, you, they are being ruled.' Later on these forms in *-minī* became tied down to the Second Person by an interesting process, as we shall see in § **319.**

Suffixes ending in Consonants

§ **242.** Suffixes ending in Consonants form Nouns of the Third Declension. The commonest are :

    -ter- : *-tr-* (*pater*)

    -tōr- (*dator*)

    -ōn- (*-ō* in Nom. Sing.) : *-en-* (generally becoming *-in-*, § **122**) as in *hom-ō, hom-in-is*

-ōn- (invariable, but -ō in Nom. Sing.) : *fullō*
' fuller,' *Nāsō* ' Long-nose '; hence -mōn-, -iōn-
-nt- in Participles (§ **234**)

-et- and -it- (*hebes, stipes*)

-tā-t- (*civitās*) and -tūt- (*virtūs*)

-c- chiefly in Feminines like *nūtr-ī-x* (§ **231**).

§ **243.** A great number of words in common use
have the very ancient Neut. suffix -es- : -os-, as *genus,
generis* (§ **186**), where the variation of the vowel of the
Suffix in different Cases is due to Ablaut (§ **73**).

Its weakest form -s- sometimes appears in derivatives as in the adjective-forming -ōsus from -od-s-us
(§ **166**) which contains the weakest form of the stem
of *odor* ' smell, fragrance '; the old nom. *odōs* was
displaced by *odōr* (later *odor*, § **130**) on the pattern of
the other Cases (§ **186**) and of the Nouns in -tor,
-tōris, where -ōr in the Nominative was original.

This lengthened form (§ **79**) of the suffix -ōs, -ōris
was masculine, not neuter, and appears in a number
of Abstract Nouns in -or, -ōris (§§ **130** and **292**).

Confusion of the Consonantal and -i- Declensions

§ **244.** Many consonantal stems, especially those
ending in -t-, have forms which properly belong to
-i- stems, e.g. the Gen. Plur. in -ium appears not only
from -i- nouns like *ovis, hostis*, but in *noct-ium, cīvitāt-
ium*, and Participles like *amantium* (older *amantum*).

Conversely the Acc. in -em which belongs to consonantal stems (for I.Eu. -m̥) as in *ped-em*, has invaded
-i- nouns like *ovem, partem* (older *ovim, partim*).

§ **245.** This was probably due largely to the forms

which had been given by phonetic changes to the gen.
sing. and the nom. and acc. plur. in the two classes
of stems.

Thus at about 250 B.C. the inflexions must have
been—as we know from other languages—

	Consonant stems	-*i*- stems
nom. plur.	*rēg-ĕs	host-ēs
acc. plur.	rēg-ēs	host-īs

the confusing difference of meaning in the long -*ēs*
ending (acc. and nom. plur.) led to a levelling of these
and other forms in the two systems. But the old
Acc. Plur. (never Nom.) in -*īs* from -*i*- stems remained
in use in poetry, so that Vergil always wrote e.g. *hostīs*,
ovīs for the Acc.

Transfer from the u- *to the* i- *Declension*

§ **246.** Note that Latin lost altogether the *u·*
Declension (§ **229**) in Adjectives; the whole of the
small but ancient group, thanks to its feminine form
(cf. Sansk. masc. *svādus*, fem. *svādvī*, ' sweet ' (Gr.
ἡδύς, ἡδεῖα) was transferred in Latin to the -*i*- declension; thus we have

    suāvis : Gr. ἡδύς

    gravis : Gr. βαρύς (§ **172**)

    levis : Gr. ἐ-λαχύς, Sans. *raghús*

    dulcis : Gr. γλυκύς, probably from *δλυκύς.

The suffix which formed the feminine in these words
shows generally (§ **71**) the forms -*iē̆-* : -*iə-* (Gr. and
Lat. -*ia*) : -*ī-*. In adjectives in Latin it was changed

to the common -*i*- suffix appearing in words like
ovis, no doubt because in some Cases (perhaps Abl.
sing. and Gen. plur.) the two Declensions had in the
earliest Latin come to have identical endings.

Meanings attached to different Suffixes

§ **247.** Denoting the A g e n t : the oldest and commonest are

  -*tōr*- masc., -*trīc*- fem. (*dator, datrix*)

  -*ōn*- (*volō* ' volunteer,' *fullō* ' fuller ').

§ **248.** Denoting the I n s t r u m e n t :

  -*mo*- and -*mā*- (*rēmus* (§ **191**) ' oar ' ; *līma* ' file,' lit.
    ' means of smoothing,' from *lino*)

  -*men* and -*mento* (*teg-men* ' covering,' from *tego ;*
    docu-mentum ' means of proving,' from *doceo*)

  -*lo*- and -*ro*- (*capu-lum, fulc-rum*)

  -*tlo*- (whence -*clo*-, *pōculum* ' cup,' § **159**) and
    -*tro*- (*arā-trum* ' plough ')

  I.Eu. -*dhlo*- and -*dhro*- (§ **177** (3)), Lat. -*blo*-,
    -*bro*- (*pati-bulum* (on the unfolded vowel
    cf. § **159**) *flā-brum*).

§ **249.** The suffixes -*mo*-, -*men*-, -*mento*-, also -*no·*
and -*nā*-, often appear added to stems ending in -*s*-
(§ **243**) ; and this -*s*- was always lost later on before
the -*m*- and -*n*- as in *rēmus, lūmen, iūmentum, lūna,*
§ **191**. We might indeed better describe the formant
in many words as a compound suffix (-*s-mo*-, -*s-men-to*-,
and the like).

§ **250.** Denoting R e l a t i o n s h i p : the only
important suffix is

  -*ter*-, -*tr*- (*pater, māter, frāter*) ; cf. § **60** (2) (a).

§ **250a.** Of P l a c e :

-tōrio-, neut. (*audi-tōrium*)

also *-clo-* (orig. *-tlo-*) and *-dhlo-*, e.g. *cubĭculum*, *sta-bulum*.

§ **251.** D i m i n u t i v e s : *-lo-* (*porcu-lus* ' little pig ') and in many derivative suffixes, *-ello-*, *-iculo-*, *-cello-*, *-bello-*, and often in the Fem. form *-ellā-*.

§ **251a.** When the Diminutive suffix is used in Adjectives, it conveys a softened meaning, e.g. *pallidulus* ' rather pale,' from *pallidus* ' pale.'

Comparative Suffixes

§ **252.** C o m p a r a t i v e s : The chief suffix was *-iōs-* : *-ios* (later *-ius*), as in e.g. *mel-ior,* where the *-r-* of the other Cases (§ **186**) has forced itself into the Nom. Masc. (earlier **meliōs*), cf. § **243.**

The weakest form (§ **67**) of this suffix was *-is-* which we see in adverbs like *mag-is, nim-is* and *pris-,* beside *prius, prior,* seen in *pris-cus, prī-mus* (§ **193**). In combination with *-tero-* it appears in *magister, minister.*

§ **253.** *-tero-* appears alone in words denoting a contrast between two—as in *al-ter, dex-ter, ex-terī* ' foreigners.' Sometimes it is compounded with *-iōr-* as in *exterior, interior ;* or added to *-is-* as in *magister* (§ **252**).

Superlative Suffixes

§ **254.** S u p e r l a t i v e s : the simplest suffixes are *-mo-* as in *sum-mus* (§ **156**) ;

H

-tomo-, later *-tumo-*, later still *-timo-* (§ **123**) as in *ul-tumus, ultimus.*

§ **255.** The *max-* of *maximus* (Old Lat. *maxomos*) contains the weakest form (§ **243**) of an I.Eu. stem **maĝh-os*, Sansk. *mahas* ' greatness.' This very common word probably set the type from which *-somos*, later *-sumus*, was taken into use as a superlative ending, hence e.g. *pessumus* for **ped-somo-s* ' nearest one's feet, lowest,' and all the superlatives in *-llimus*, *-rrimus*, where *-ll-, -rr-* have come from *-ls-, -rs-* (§ **190**) ; **acer-sumo-* had come from **acri-somo-*, § **128**. On the vowel of the penult see § **123**.

§ **256.** The ordinary *-issumo-*, *-issimo-* (§ **123**) seems to be an addition of this *-sumo-* to the comparative *-is-* (§ **252**) just as in *magis-ter*, and in the Greek superlative ending *-ισ-τος*, occasionally *-ίσ-τατος*.

Numeral Suffixes

§ **257.** O r d i n a l s show the suffixes *-to-* and *-mo-* (*quartus, decimus*); in *tertius* we have the compound *-tio-.*

Distributive Numerals

§ **258.** D i s t r i b u t i v e s. These curious adjectives, *bini, terni,* and the rest, meaning generally ' two apiece,' ' three apiece ' and so on, arose from Neuter Nouns like **bīnum* ' a pair,' **ternum* ' a set of three.' But these nouns were turned into adjectives so that instead of saying **bīnum pōmōrum* ' a pair of apples,' one said *bīna pōma* ' apples in a pair,' and hence ' apples in pairs,' ' two apples each.' A trace of

the older use survives in the common poetic idiom
by which these Adjectives are used in the Sing. to
mean ' a set of (so many),' e.g. Vergil's *centena arbor*
' a set of a hundred tree-stems (turned into oars).'

Other Adjectival Suffixes

§ **259.** The very common and ancient suffix *-io-* has
many uses, all derived from the meaning ' belonging
to,' ' connected with ' as in *patrius* ' belonging to our
fathers ' or ' to a father ' ; see also § **262.**

§ **260.** The suffix *-co-* had a similar meaning, but
it is rare in Latin (*hosticus, cīvicus*).

§ **261.** On the adjectival suffix *-ōso-* see § **243** ;
-ulento- had the same meaning, if it is for *-olento-*
from *oleo*, see §§ **122, 123.**

§ **262.** The Suffixes *-lo-, -vo-, -io-, -so-*, and the
compound *-tīvo-* often show Participial meanings,
as in *pendu-lus* ' hanging,' *vī-vu-s* ' living,' *ar-vum*
' ploughed land ' ; *ex-im-ius* (from *ex-imo*) ' taken
out, choice, rare ' ; *devexus* ' moving down, inclining '
(from *veho*), cf. *fluxus, flexus, alsus ; in-si-tīvus* (from
insero) ' grafted.'

§ **263.** A suffix that arose in Latin is *-ēnsis*, denoting
persons or things belonging to a particular place,
generally some town in Italy, as *Arīminēnsis* ' belonging
to, coming from Ariminum.' This probably arose from
the old Genitive of certain place names ending in *-ō*,
-ōnis, as *Furfens* gen. of *Furfō ;* though probably
this particular genitive form ought to be called rather
Sabine than Old Latin, since the inscription on which
it appears is from Sabine country. From such names

it spread in soldiers' and country folk's talk to other words like *castrēnsis*, *arvēnsis*, all such forms implying to start with a half-playful metaphor, the farmer describing some weed as a ' citizen of the ploughed field.'

§ **264.** Another local suffix which may have been of genuine Latin origin, though springing up outside Rome in the country towns, is -*ās*, -*ātis*, as in *Aufidēnās* ' a native of Aufidena,' *Arpīnās* ' a native of Arpinum.'

Formation of Adverbs

§ **265.** With the possible exception of a few ancient monosyllables like *prŏ* ' before,' Adverbs were all originally Cases of Nouns, either alone or attached to a Preposition, as may be clearly seen in such Latin adverbs as *iūre* ' with right, lawfully ' (Abl.), or *modo* ' only ' (§ **16**), or *ob iter* ' on the way, in passing,' *dēnuō* (§ **135**) from *dē-novō* ' from a fresh (beginning), afresh.'

§ **266.** Many arose from different uses of the Ablative. Besides those like *iūre* and *modo*, in which the Abl. is Instrumental, we have the Abl. Neut. of Participles used in an Abstract sense, as *auspicātō* ' with auspices duly taken,' *compositō* ' by arrangement, by contrivance,' all from the same Instrumental meaning of the Case. The Abl. of Measure gives us *multō* ' by far ' and others, used with words expressing a comparison. The Abl. of Time-when gives *prīmō* ' at first '; the Abl. of Manner or Line-by-which gives *quā* ? ' by what road ? ' But *dextrā* ' on the right,' *illā* ' there ' ' by that road,' and others like them, may be mainly Abl. of Place where.

§ **267.** Most adjectives of the Second Declension have what is probably an old Instrumental Case in -*ē* with Adverbial meaning, e.g. *lātus* ' wide,' gives *lātē* ' widely,' *sānus* ' sane,' gives *sānē* ' soundly, seriously, quite.'

§ **268.** Many come from the Accusative of Extent as *multum* ' much '; *parum* (earlier *parvom*, § **146**) ' little, too little.'

§ **269.** A large number in -*tim*, -*sim* came from Nouns formed with -*ti*-, as *partim* (the older Accusative of *pars*, § **244**) ' to the extent of a part, partly.' Many of these preserve the Acc. of the old Verbal Abstract Nouns which had otherwise (§ **216**) died out, e.g. *statim* lit. ' during one's standing,' i.e. ' at once,' *summātim* (from *summāre* ' to sum up ') ' by way of summing up, briefly.'

On the pattern of such Adverbs the suffix -*ātim* came to be used even where there was no Verb in -*āre*, as in *gradātim* ' step by step,' *paullātim* ' little by little.' Most of the Adverbs from Comparative Adjectives like *plēnius* ' more fully, to a fuller extent,' *altius* ' more highly,' are probably also Accusatives of the same kind. But some may be Nominative (v. § **272** inf.).

§ **270.** The Acc. *iter* attached itself to many Adjectives (e.g. *breviter, longiter, largiter*) just like the Eng. *way* in ' straightway,' and this became the regular formation from Adjectives of the Third Declension, though the Acc. Sing. neut. is used in some, e.g. *facile* ' easily.'

§ **271.** Many Adverbs arise from the Nominative,

sometimes because an Adj. or Partc. originally agreeing
with the subject of the sentence came to be felt detached,
like the Eng. participles *excepting, considering, seeing
that*. Thus *miles abiit, domum versus* meant originally
' the soldier went away, turning homewards ' ; and
from such uses the last two words came to mean
simply ' towards home,' and the word *versus* used,
whatever the subject might have been, merely as
a Preposition, or rather a Post-position. So *praeceps*
' headlong,' *prōrsus* ' set forward, going on,' hence
' thoroughly, completely,' were to start with Nominatives.

§ 272. Sometimes the Nominative was originally
a parenthetic statement, e.g. *primum* ' the first time
(was, is, will be) ' ; *deinceps* ' the next following event
(was, is, will be),' and so simply as adverbs meaning
' for the first time,' ' next.' So in English ' *the first
thing*,' ' *no fear*,' ' *not a bit*,' ' *nay more*.' Some of the
Comparative adverbs may have been Nominativ,es :
melius ' it is (or ' was ' or ' will be ') better,' *amplius*
' there is more too, and more.' This is probably how
amplius came to be used with numerals without
quam (*ducenti amplius* ' two hundred and more ') ;
then when its adverbial meaning was established it
came to be put in front of the numeral as qualifying it,
amplius ducenti ' liberally two hundred ' ; and the
custom of omitting *quam* spread to *minus* also.

NOTE ON PRONOUNS

§ 273. Any treatment of the Morphology of the Pronouns
has been deliberately excluded from the scope of this book.

It is one of the most difficult parts of Indo-European Philology, and its discussion requires a wide range of acquaintance with the earliest recorded forms of many languages. At the same time it is also somewhat unremunerative; that is to say, it is rarely possible to discover anything more than we know from the separate languages of the meaning and use of the various stems involved.

But the reason for this is interesting. The Personal Pronouns go back to an immeasurable antiquity. Number, Gender, Case, Nouns, Verbs—all these are things on which the Pronouns might look down with contempt as childish novelties; the Pronouns existed long before any of these things were dreamt of. *I*, *me*, *thou*, *we*, *us*, *you*, *he*, *it*, *they*, and their equivalents in Indo-European, are no parts of any system—they are all distinct w o r d s o f w h o l l y s e p a r a t e o r i g i n—rough, indigestible fragments of speech which the grammatical instinct of later ages in vain sought to assimilate into a coherent system, though it did succeed to some extent in plastering their rough corners;—as when the primitive Greek *ἀσμε* (Lesbian *ἄμμε*) ' us ' —whose first syllable is closely connected with Eng. *us*, Germ. *uns*, and with Lat. *nōs*—was made in Ionic Greek to look like a respectable plural by the addition of -*as*, and more like a Pronoun by the prefixion of the rough breathing in imitation of the *ὑ-* proper to the Second Person. Thus, by various phonetic changes, arose Attic *ἡμᾶς*.

But a few points of interest which happen also to be certain in the history of the Latin Pronouns have been dealt with in §§ 105, 147, 190, 192, 212.

B. THE SHAPING OF VERBS

Stem of the Present Indicative

§ **274.** In all branches of Indo-European we find traces of two different ways of forming what is called the Present Stem. At the time when the Eastern segment (Indo-Persian, Armenian, and Slavonic) began to separate from the rest, far the largest number of Verbs had a vowel (-*e*- or -*o*-) immediately preceding the endings of the different Persons, and so separating them from the root. This vowel is most clearly preserved in Greek forms like λέγ-ο-μεν 'we say,' λέγ-ε-τε 'ye say'; in Latin, through the degradation of unaccented Vowels (§ 122), both appear merely as -*i*- (*leg-i-mus, leg-i-tis*).

§ 275. This vowel is called the Theme-vowel and all forms which show it are called Thematic. It is often combined with some other formative element, as in the Present-suffixes:

-*i̯o*- : -*i̯e*-, -*no*- : -*ne*-, -*sk̂o*- : -*sk̂e*-, -*to*- : -*te*-, -*so*- : -*se*-.

Examples of these in Latin are:

cap-iō : the Partc. *cap-tus*
li-nō : ,,   ,,   *li-tus*
nō-scō : ,,   ,,   *nō-tus*
plec-to : Gr. πλέκ-ω (cf. Lat. *plico*, which is a De-composite from *explico, complico*, §§ 21, 122)
vīso (for **vid-so*) : *vid-eo*.

But all these Presents are equally Thematic, *i.e.* they all show the Theme-vowel.

§ 276. The difference between the forms with -*o*- and those with -*e*- is no doubt due to some conditions of Ablaut (§ 73) in the parent language which we have not enough evidence to define. And there is no reason to doubt the original identity of this Theme-Vowel with what we call the -*e*- : -*o*- suffix of the Second Declension (§ 226). So if we go back far enough, the stem of *coquos* 'cook' and *coquō* 'I cook' were the same (cf. also *fīdus* ' trust-worthy ' : *fīdo* ' I trust ' or Gr. *ἄγω* ' I drive ' : *ἀγός* ' driver, leader '). But in the Verb the stem was followed by the endings of Person, in the Noun by the endings of Case.

§ 277. In the other, and no doubt much older, class of Presents, there is no Theme-vowel, and the Personal endings follow the Root-syllable immediately, as in Lat. *es-t* ' is,' *es-tis* ' ye are ' (contrast *reg-i-t*, *reg-i-tis*), *fer-t* ' bears,' *volt* ' wishes,' *da-mus*, *da-tis*, *da-nt*, ' we (you, they) give ' (§ 71). This class is called Non-Thematic ; and it has left far more numerous examples in Greek (e.g. *φη-μί* ' I say,' *τί-θη-μι* ' I place ') and Sanskrit (*ád-mi* ' I eat,' cf. Lat. *ēs-tis* ' you eat,' *ēs-t* ' he eats '). But in Latin all except a very few of the forms in most common use, such as those just quoted, have been ' levelled ' into the Thematic class. Hence beside *est* ' he eats ' we have the First Pers. *edō* ' I eat.' The only Present Indic. that retains the Non-Thematic *-m* in the First Person is *sum* ' I am ' (older **som*) ; for *inquam* was probably originally a Present Subjunc. meaning ' let me say,' though it came to be used as the First Pers. corresponding to *inquis, inquit,* which belong to the regular Thematic type.

§ 278. In these old Non-Thematic verbs, note that the Theme-vowel is absent also from their Infinitives ; contrast *es-se, vel-le, fer-re* (§ 190) with *reg-ere*, older **reg-ese* (§ 186). So in the Impf. Subj. (*es-sem, vel-lem*, but *reg-e-rem*).

§ 279. Observe also that the Present Subjunctive of these Non-Thematic Verbs was in Latin formed with the ' optative ' suffix *-iē-* : *-ī-*, *sīm* (Old Lat. *siēm*), *simus*, *velim*, *edim*. But in *fero*, and later in *edo*, the *-ā-* (§ **283**) of the regular Thematic Subjunctive came into use. In this as in other Tenses of its ' Subjunctive ' Latin has completely run into one the two Indo-European Moods which in Greek are still distinct as ' Conjunctive ' and ' Optative.'

§ **280.** The true Conjunctive corresponding to these Non-thematic Indicatives was formed by adding the theme-vowel itself, as in Greek, Indic. ἴ-μεν ' we go,' Conjunctive (in Homer) ἴ-ομεν ' let us go, we are to go ' ; or in Ion. ἔω (from ἐσ-ω) ' let me be, I am to be,' Att. ὦ, which exactly corresponds (§ **186**) to Lat. *ero* which is used as a Future, just as ἔδομαι from the root of *edo* was in Greek (§ **164**). But in later Greek the stem-vowels of the Conjunctives like ἴομεν, ἴετε were lengthened to match those of Conjunctives like λέγωμεν, λέγητε formed from Thematic Presents (λέγομεν, λέγετε).

§ **281.** Examples of the commonest types of simple Thematic presents have been already given (*regō, capiō, linō, nōscō*). But the *-io-* class was more widely used in Latin than at first we realise, because to it belong not merely the 4th Conjugation (*audiō*), but also the 1st and 2nd, in which to start with the *-io-* followed a vowel and the *-i̯-* was lost (§ **136**). Thus e.g. *moneo* comes from **mon-ei̯o ; laudās* is contracted for **lauda-i̯es, monēs* for **mon-ei̯es ;* probably also *laudō* for **laudāi̯o, laudant* for **laudāi̯ont*. But **moneont*, which would not have been contracted, was replaced by *monent*, on the pattern of *-āmus*

: -*ant* in the *ā*- Verbs. The differences between the *audio* and the *capio* class have been explained in § 97.

Enough has now been said to show the general relation of the Personal endings to the original Present-stems ; to enter into further detail as to these endings would lead us to discuss a great number of not very important riddles, on many of which we have at present too little evidence for any decision.

§ 282. Two other classes of Thematic Present-stems in Indo-European are represented by a few common Verbs in Latin, namely,

(1) Presents formed by an ' Infixed Nasal ' as in

> *linquo* : *līquī, -lictum.*
> *rumpo* : *rūpī, ruptum.*
> *findo* : *fidī, fissum.*

Cf. Gr. λαμβάνω, Ion. Fut. λάμψομαι, beside Aor. ἔ-λαβον.

(2) Presents formed by Reduplication (in Indo-European the Vowel of the Reduplicating syllable in the Present was -*i*-), as

> *gi-gn-o* : Partc. *gen-itus.*
> *si-st-o* : Partc. *sta-tus* (§ 71).
> *si-so, later *sero* (§§ 186, 99) : Partc. *sa-tus* (§ 71).

In the last two examples a Non-Thematic Present (Gr. ἵ-η-μι,[1] earlier *si-sē-mi) has been converted in Latin into the ordinary Thematic type.

---

[1] But this Greek verb is a ' portmanteau-word,' i.e. it is two words packed into one. One, meaning ' to set, put,' is identical with Lat. *sero ;* the other, meaning ' to hurl, cast,' is from the simpler form of the root seen in Lat. *iacio,* cf. Lat. perf. *iēcī* with Gr. Aor. ἧκ-α, § 71.

Tenses derived from Present Stems

§ **283.** From the Present Indicative were derived the different forms of the Present Subjunctives, with one of two suffixes *-ē-* and *-ā-*, both of which are found in other languages. And the Impf. Subj. in *-rem*, earlier *-sēm* (§ **186**), whatever its origin, was in any case based ultimately on the Present stem.

§ **284.** From the Present-stem came also the Imperfect Indicative in all Conjugations, by means of the Formant *-bā-* (older *-fu̯ā-*, § **150**), which was added to a form of the stem (*laudā-, monē-, regē, audiē-*) whose function is not quite certain, but which in some one of the forms which set the type for the rest must have been felt as a kind of Infinitive, e.g. *monē-bam* (if that was the earliest type) 'I was in warning,' 'I was a-warning.'

§ **285.** Similarly was formed the Future Indicative in the *ā-* and *ē-* Conjugations (*laudābō, monēbō*), and also, in Old Latin, in the *ī-* Conjugation (§ **286**). In all these *-bō* comes from *-fu̯ō* (§ **150**), an old Future from the root which appears in *fuī*; or more precisely, an old Conjunctive, like *ero*, see § **280**.

§ **286.** In the Third Conjugation, the Future shows *-ā-* in the 1st Person Sing. and *-ē-* in the others—both properly Conjunctive endings; the reason for the difference in the 1st Pers. Sing. is not yet quite certain. The Fourth Conjugation followed this type in Ciceronian Latin, but in Plautus we have often *audībō* and the like, following *monēbō*.

Meanings of the Present-Stems

§ **287.** All the different Present-formations came into Latin with the notions of Continuous, Repeated, or Habitual action in Present time. Besides this a few special types of meaning and form should be noted.

§ **288.** I n c e p t i v e meaning (' to begin to . . . ') is especially common in the verbs in *-scō*, as e.g. *crēbrēscere* ' to begin to be frequent.'

§ **289.** F r e q u e n t a t i v e meaning appears in the 1st Conj. verbs in *-tāre, -itāre, -titāre*, e.g. *dictāre*, ' to go on saying, dictate,' *flāgitāre* ' to ask over and over again,' *dictitāre* ' to say repeatedly, make a point of saying.'

§ **290.** A c t i t i v e and F a c t i t i v e (also called C a u s a t i v e) meanings are common in *ā-* Verbs derived from nouns, e.g. (1) Actitive : *exulāre* ' to be an exile ' from *exul ; equitāre* ' to be a horseman, display horsemanship ' ; *domināri* ' to play the master, act as a tyrant.'

(2) Factitive : *dēnsāre* ' to make dense,' from *dēnsus ; fugāre* ' to put into flight ' from *fuga ; exāmināre* ' to put on the scale, weigh ' from *exāmen ; armāre* ' to provide with armour ' from *arma*.

§ **291.** D e s c r i p t i o n or P a s s i v e C o n - d i t i o n is often expressed by verbs in *-ēre*, e.g.

> *iacēre* ' be lying, be cast down ' beside the Active *iacere* ' to cast ' (cf. § **282** footn.).
>
> *pendēre* ' be hanging, suspended ' beside the Active *pendere* ' to suspend.'
>
> *rubēre* ' to be red, blush ' (cf. § **177** (2)).
>
> *splendēre* ' to shine brightly,' and many more.

§ 292. It is worth noting that these Intransitives in *-ēre* often had associated with them Abstract Nouns in *-or* (older *-ōs* (§ **243**)), *-ōris*, and Adjectives in *-idus*, as

> *splendeō, splendor, splendidus*
> *squāleō, squālor, squālidus.*

§ 293. Some of the Verbs in *-eo*, however, like *moneo* ' I put in mind, warn,' from the Deflected (§ **73**) form of the root seen in *mens* (§ **92**) and *meminī* (from **memen-ī*, § **122**), were F a c t i t i v e in meaning all along. They contained the Present Suffix *-ei̯o-*, whereas the Intransitives described in § **291** were derived from *-ēi̯o-* ; but by Phonetic changes (§§ **106, 136**) both became simply *-eo-* in Latin. The same double origin appears in Greek *-ei̯o-* verbs ; φιλεῖν ' to treat as a friend ' (Factitive) beside e.g. ῥῑγεῖν ' to be cold ' (Descriptive).

§ 294. A few Verbs in *-īre* denote a m o r b i d condition of body or mind, as *insānīre* ' to be mad,' *garrīre* ' to be a chatterbox ' ; also *gestīre* ' to be over desirous,' and *formīdo* from an obsolete **formīre* (from *formus* ' warm ') ' to turn hot and cold, shudder,' § **181** (1). The ending of *glūtīre* ' to be a glutton ' may have been imitated in *balbūtīre* ' to be a stammerer,' and one or two other verbs.

The joints of the Perfect Stem

§ 295. The Latin Active Perfect Tense is a remarkable ' conflation ' of at least four different Indo-European Tense-forms, the Perfect Active and Middle, and the Aorist, Active and Middle ; and more than one type of Aorist has been pressed into the mixture. The fusion of Tenses appears clearly also in the double use of the Perfect; *dīxī* means both ' I said ' and ' I have said.'

§ **296.** The endings *-ī* and *-tī* in the Sing. and perhaps *-re* in the Plural seem from their nearest parallels in Sanskrit to have been proper to the Middle Voice (cf. § **308**). But the endings *-it* and *-unt, -mus* and *-tis* are Active.

§ **297.** Perfects like *tutudī, pupugī* show the Reduplication of the Indo-European Perfect, but with the vowel of the reduplicating-syllable matching that of the root-syllable, not *-e-* as in Greek (e.g. Gr. πέποιθα from πείθω) ; but this *-e-* appears in forms like *pepulī*, and Old Latin *tetulī*, later *tulī* (§ **89**).

§ **298.** Many Perfects like *fidī, tulī, tendī* (in Plautus *tetulī, tetendī*) were originally reduplicated but have lost their first syllable through the influence of the form to which the Perfect was reduced in their compounds (*contulī, diffidī,* and so on), where the short unaccented syllable was lost by the regular syncope (§ **89**).

§ **299.** Perfects like *cēpī, lēgī, frēgī* seem to have been made on the type of those like *ēmī, ēgī*, whose first syllable seems to have contained the *e-* of reduplication contracted with the vowel (*e* or *a*) of the root-syllable, just as does e.g. Gr. ἦγμαι ' I have been led,' the Perf. Pass. of ἄγω. No doubt *fēcī* helped (§ **71**).

§ **300.** Perfects like *rēxī, vāsī* (for the long *-ē-* and *-ā-* see § **108**) contain the ordinary *-s-* of the Aorist tense as in Gr. ἔ-λεξ-α from the root *leg-* (λέγω) ; and apart from the Greek Augment, the Greek 3rd pers. sing. ἔ-δειξ-ε, earlier *ἐ-δειξ-ετ, very closely resembles Lat. *dīxit*.

§ **301.** Perfects in *-vī* were developed in the *ā-* and *ē-* and *ī-* Conjugations (*amāvī, flēvī, audīvī*), probably on the pattern of words like

$$\left. \begin{array}{l} \text{Perf. } m\bar{o}v\bar{\imath} : \text{Partc. } m\bar{o}tus \\ \quad\ f\bar{o}v\bar{\imath} : \quad\ \text{,,} \quad\ f\bar{o}tus \end{array} \right\} \ \S\,144$$

from the participles *amātus, flētus, audītus*.

Then **moně-vī* (with *-ě-* see § **293**) became *monuī* (§ **135**), and *audīvī* became *audiī* (§ **107**); but the old form in *-īvī* was restored beside *audiī* by the same analogy of the Partc. in *-ītus* (with *mōvī* : *mōtus*) as had first created it, so that both the forms were in use.

§ **302.** In the 2nd Pers. Sing. and Plur. the curious formants *-is-* and *-sis-* appear as in *vic-is-tī-, scrīp-sis-tī;* these contain longer forms of the Aorist suffix which it is impossible to discuss further here. But forms like *dīxtī, amāstī* have every right to be considered more primitive; just as the old Lat. Perf. Inf. *dīxe* is more primitive than *dīxisse*. Forms like *dīxtī, dīxe* could not have arisen by contraction since the syllable *-is-* in *dīxistī, dīxisse* was accented, see § **85** (4); and in any contraction or syncope it is the accented syllable that is (not lost but) preserved.

Tenses derived from the Perfect

§ **303.** The Pluperfect is derived from the Perfect stem by an Aorist suffix *-es-ā-*, later (§ **186**) *-erā-* (for the *-ā-* compare that of the Impf. in *-bām*, § **284**). In both tenses, as in *eram*, the Imperfect of *esse*, the original meaning of the *-ā-*, and its relation to the *-ā-* of the Subjunctive (§ **283**), are problems which there is at present very little evidence to solve.

§ **304.** The Future Perfect is really a Conjunctive of the *-es-* Aorist, closely parallel to the Conjunctive, which in Latin served as a Future Indic., of the verb *es-* ' to be,' **esō*, later *ero* (see § **280**).   This Conjunctive of Non-Thematic Verbs was originally inflected in exactly the same way as the Pres. Indic. of Thematic Verbs, so *ero* is inflected like *rego*.

§ **305.** But in the Future Perfect the ending of the 3rd Pers. Plural was changed to *-rint*, to match the *-rimus*, *-ritis* of the other two Persons, and to avoid a likeness with the *-runt* of the Perf. Indic.   In *-ris, -rimus*, *-ritis* of the Fut. Perf. the *-i-* is short, just as in *eris*, *regis*.

§ **306.** The Perfect Subjunctive is an Aorist Optative— *-es-ī-* becoming *-er-ī-* (§ **186**)—and shows the same Optative stem as *sim* (§ **279**).   In these forms the *-ī-* is properly long (except before final *-t*, § **130**), but the poets occasionally make it short by confusion with the Future Perfect forms.

§ **307.** The Pluperfect Subjunctive is clearly derived from the Perfect stem, and contains some kind of Aorist Subjunctive or Optative, shaped by analogy with *essem*.   The parallelism between the relation of the Impf. Subj. to the Pres. Inf., and that of the Plupf. Subj. to the Perf. Inf. cannot be accidental, but nothing more than this can be said with any degree of probability.

Passives and Deponents

§ **308.** In pro-ethnic Indo-European, besides the Active inflexions, there existed a whole system of parallel forms which we call the ' Middle ' Voice from the name given to them in Greek. The Middle forms seem to have denoted a state or movement or feeling of the subject of the Verb, or some action in which he was more than usually interested, such as an action done to himself, or for his own profit. This complexity of meaning has descended into Latin, so that it uses the same inflexions in Passive and Deponent Verbs ; but the inflexions themselves underwent drastic analogical changes in the period before Latin became a separate language, while its speakers were hardly, if at all, separated from the speakers of what at a slightly later stage we call Keltic.

§ **309.** The only original Middle form preserved was the 2nd Pers. Sing. of the Imperative (e.g. *sequere* ' follow '), and even in that phonetic changes (§§ **105, 186**) had taken place ; the same form appears in Old Latin in the 2nd Pers. of the Present Indicative (*sequere* thou followest ') ; but later on, an *-s* was added to mark this as Indic., hence *sequeris* (§ **122**). Besides this may be mentioned the Middle-Passive Participial form in *-minī*, see § **241**.

§ **310.** In some other Middle or Passive forms final *-r* was added to the original Middle form, as in e.g. the 3rd Sg. and Plu., *sequitur, sequontur* (*-tor* was probably the earlier form in both, cf. § **127**) instead of I.Eu. **seqeto, *seqonto* (with what we call in Greek

' secondary endings,' i.e. those which in Greek appear in Past Tenses). In others the *-r* was added to the Active form (*rego-r*) or substituted for the final sound of the Active (*regimur* instead of *regimus*).

§ **311.** The origin of this curious *-r* which appears both in Latin (as well as the kindred dialects Oscan and Umbrian) and in Keltic was discovered in 1889. In some tenses of the I.Eu. Active Verb the ending *-r* was an alternative ending to the *-nt* or *-nti* of the 3rd Plur., so that, e.g., a form like **bheror* could mean 'they carry.' In Irish, in Welsh, and in Osco-Umbrian such forms are used with an Accusative to form a rudimentary kind of Passive, as Ir. *-m berar* ' I am carried,' lit. ' folk carry me,' Welsh *-m dysgir* ' I am taught,' lit. ' folk teach me.'

In Latin the origin of this use was forgotten and a new true Passive (with the Object of the action in the Nominative as the Subject of the Verb) formed by amalgamating this rudimentary form with the old Middle inflexion, as we have seen in § **310.**

§ **312.** The only trace left in Latin of this early meaning of the Passive forms, but an important trace, is the great fondness which appears in all Latin writers for what is called the ' Impersonal ' Passive, which exhibits, as we now see, the proper and original use of the *r-* forms. Uses like *itur* ' folk go,' ' they go,' *curritur* ' they run,' reflect the old idiom more truly than such ' developed ' Passives as *dux capitur* ' the chief is taken.'

§ **313.** The use of the 3rd Pers. Sing. of the Perfect Passive tenses with the Participle in the Neuter arose to match the Impersonal use of other tenses, from the fact that the Neuter of the Partc. in -*tus* had always been used as an Abstract Verbal Noun (cf. the Adverbs like *compositō* (§ **266**), so that *ventum est* ' there is an arrival, folk have come ' seemed a perfectly straightforward and natural form of speech.

§ **314.** All that was needed to make *ventum est* mean ' folk came ' was the same shift of meaning, from a pure Present Perfect to an Aorist, which had taken place in the Masc. and Fem. forms ; *captus est* originally meant ' he is a prisoner, he has been taken ' ; but it came to be used to mean ' he was taken ' just as Germ. *er hat es gemacht*, Fr. *il l'a fait*, both often mean ' he did it.' This shift of meaning was all the easier because of the fusion of Aorist and Perfect into one tense in the Active (§ **295**) ; but it may be rather that this fusion in the Active was helped by the double use of the Passive Perfect forms, which may have grown up first.

Infinitives Active and Passive

§ **315.** Since the Infinitive was originally a Case (Dat. or Loc.) of a Verbal Noun, it was properly neither Active nor Passive. But when the idiom of the Acc. and Inf. had grown up in Latin to represent in Indirect Speech a statement with the Indicative in Direct Speech, it was felt necessary to make some distinction in the form of the Infinitive for Active and Passive.

§ **316.** Forms like *agī* (Dat. of a Root-noun or Loc. of an *o*-noun) (§ **224**), and *agere* (Loc.), *fierī* (Dat.) of an *es*-noun (§ **243**), must in Old Latin have competed with one another in use, all expressing much the same idea, ' for ' or ' in ' the action denoted by the Verb. Hence arose by what is called ' Contamination ' or ' Conflation ' combined forms like *agier, regier,* if, as seems most probable, they have lost a final *-e* by Syncope in a sentence (§§ **91**, **92**) and stand for **agi-ere, regi-ere.* They were naturally assigned to the Passive because of their final *-r* (§ **311**). Then the forms in *-ere* (§ **186**), by contrast with them, came to be felt to be Active ; and as these forms seem to have been always more frequently used than those in *-ī*, so that their Active meaning was familiar and fixed, the forms in *-ī* by contrast came to be assigned to the Passive, and the *-ī* to be counted as a Passive ending. This account of the development of the Infinitive as part of the Verbal system is necessarily somewhat conjectural ; but since we know certainly that the forms were Cases to start with, some such rough-and-ready differentiation must have taken place.

§ **317.** Hence Dative forms like *amārī, monērī* (contracted from *-ăi̯erī, -ei̯erī*, § **136**) were counted Passive too. The form *-erī* with *-ĕ-*, which we should expect from Verbs of the Third Conjugation, only held its own in the word *fīō*, which has a Passive meaning ; it probably remained here because it was felt to be much clearer than **fī*, which is what the simpler form **fī-ī* must have become. In all other Verbs of this Conjugation the simple *-ī* in the end prevailed, as in *regī*.

§ **318.** The use of the old Infinitive in *-minī* (Gr. *-μεναι*), properly a Dat. from a Verbal noun in *-men*, e.g. *regiminī* (properly Dat. of *regimen*) as 2nd plur. Imperative Pass., arose first from the old Indo-European use, which appears in many languages, of the Infinitive in an Imperative sense.

Compare such Eng. phrases as ' To horse ! ' ' To the fight ! ' meaning ' Take to your horses,' ' Hurry to the fight.'

Then it was confused in sound with the Nom. Plur. Masc. and Fem. of the old Partc. with the suffix *-meno-* (§ **241**). Thus *regiminī* in Old Latin meant either ' be ruled,' ' you must be ruled,' or ' being ruled ' or if *sunt* was understood ' they are being ruled.'

§ **319.** This confusion affected the meaning of the form in two ways. Used as an Imperative in addressing one or more persons, it was of course always 2nd Person ; used as a Participle or in a statement it was Plural. Hence it came to be felt both as always 2nd Pers. and always Plural ; but it might be either Indicative or Imperative.

For the phonetic changes by which the orig. *-emenai* (Inf.) as in Homeric ἐλπέμεναι ' to hope ') *-omenoi*, *-omenai* (Partc. M. and F. Plur.) all became *-iminī* see §§ **122**, **131-2**.

The Perfect Infinitive

§ **320.** The Perfect Infinitive Active was formed from the stem of the Perfect Indicative in Early Latin by analogy with the Present Infinitive.

Thus *fuisse* was made beside *fuistī, fuistis,* as *esse* beside *estis.*

Then the relation of *fuisse* : *fuī* set the type.   There was also an old Aor. Inf. *dīxe, rēxe,* no doubt a Locative (cf. Gr. Aor. δεῖξ-αι and the like which are Datives), which when *dīxtī* (§ **302**) was extended to *dīxistī,* followed suit and was expanded to *dīxisse.*   So the form in -*isse* was commended by more than one pattern.

Future Infinitive

§ **321.** The Future Infinitive Active has been explained in §§ **187** and **225**; but see also p. 126.

§ **322.** The Future Infinitive Passive consists of the Impersonal Infinitive Passive of *īre* ' to go,' i.e. *īrī* ' that there is a going '—for the Fut. Inf. is used only in Oratio Obliqua and so must be rendered in English by a ' that '- clause—combined with the ' Acc. of Motion to ' from the Verbal Noun in -*tu*- (§ **229**) generally called the ' Supine in -*um*.'

So *captum iri* properly means ' that there is a going to take,' i.e. ' that folk will take.'   The Acc. that follows when the Verb has a Transitive meaning is the Acc. of the O b j e c t, n o t of the Subject, of the Infinitive.   Thus while with the Fut. Inf. Act. a verb like *apparet* can be used either personally or impersonally, with the Fut. Inf. Pass. it can be used only impersonally.

Thus *apparet hostes urbem mox capturos esse* or *apparent hostes urbem mox capturi esse* are both grammatical Latin, but in the Passive only *apparet urbem mox captum iri.*

ADDENDA

1 (to § 4).

THE Balto-Slavonic group includes in the Baltic half, Lithuanian and Lettish; and in the Slavonic half, Polish, Czech, Russian, Bulgarian and Serbian; the oldest form of this half is represented by Old Church Slavonic, into which the Bishops Cyril and Methodius translated the Bible in the Ninth Century A.D.; this is often cited merely as 'Slavonic.'

2 (to § 53). *Note on Whisper*

When the vocal edges are moved near to one another, so as to come in the way of the current of air, but are not stretched, the faint sound that they cause is called ' whisper '; thus Eng. *h* may be defined as a whisper preceding a voiced sound. There are no other whispered sounds in Greek, Latin or English—unless for confidential purposes we intentionally use Whisper instead of Voice.

3 (to § 187). *Note on the old Latin Fut. Inf. in* -ūrum

The explanation of this form given in § **187** is due to Dr. J. P. Postgate, who in 1890 first drew attention to the indeclinable use; and it was adopted by Brugmann *(Grundr. d. Vergl. Gramm.* Ed. 1 1892, II. p. 1268), who however later on *(Grundr.* Ed. 2 (1916), Vol. II. Part 3, p. 507) inclined to another and perhaps slightly more probable view. According to this the form in *-ūrum* is an abstract Verbal noun, to which we have parallel feminine forms in the Verbal nouns in *-ūra (pictūra, statūra),* and was originally used without any subject, so that for instance *prōmittit ventūrum* meant literally 'he promises a coming, promises to come.' Then the original character of the form was forgotten, as the Acc. and Inf. construction came more and more into favour, and an Acc. was added to express the doer of the action, until finally the *-ūrum* form, as we have seen in § **187,** was made declinable and *esse* was added.

The reasons for preferring this view are :

(1) that we have no other trace in Latin of such Inf. forms in *-om* (or later *-um*) as Postgate's explanation assumes ;

(2) that we need not separate the Inf. in *-(t)ūrum* from the Nouns in *-(t)ūra* but derive both from the Verbal Noun in *-tu-* (§ **229**) ;

(3) especially that Brugmann's explanation explains very

well the frequent omission of *sē* with the Fut. Partc. used alone without *esse* as the Fut. Inf., e.g. by Livy in *precibus aliquid mōtūrum rous* ' thinking he would prevail in some degree by entreaties ' (see Roby, *Lat. Gram.* II. § 1347) ; for we can then regard all such examples as unconscious survivals of the original construction. If a general impression based on my own reading is to be trusted, this omission of *sē* is commoner with the Fut. Partc. than with either the Pres. or Perf. Inf. ; but I do not know of any collection of evidence on the matter.

4 (to § 232). *On the use of the Acc. with the Partc. in* -tus

From the double use of the -*tus* forms noticed in this section arose a pretty idiom greatly loved by the Augustan poets but often puzzling to beginners in Latin ; namely the use of a Passive Participle with an Accusative which describes a part of the person, clothing, or armour, or some other thing essentially involved in the description (e.g. Vergil's *flōrēs inscriptī nōmina rēgum* ' flowers having kings' names traced upon them ').

NOTE.—This half-active use was preserved and extended by the poets largely because they felt that in this way they were making at home in Latin the Greek use of the Middle Voice ; phrases like *vestem succinctus* ' having his robe girt about him ' followed the type of e.g. κροκωτὸν ἠμφιεσμένη ' having put on a saffron cloak ' ; those like *oculōs dēfixa* ' having her eyes fixed upon the ground,' or *trāiectus pedēs* ' having had his feet pierced,' or *ictus femur* ' having been wounded in the thigh,' were modelled on e.g. βοστρύχους κεκαρμένη ' having had her locks cut short,' or συντετριμμένος τὴν κεφαλήν ' with his head battered.'

The use of the Acc. with an Adj., to denote parts of the body (*saucia pectus* ' wounded in the breast ') is described by Quintilian (9. 3. 17) as a Grecism which had by his day been taken even into official use (*in Actis quoque*). But how far the Latin poets thought of this construction as analogous to that with Participles it is not easy to say.

5 (to § 283). *On the origin of the Imperfect Subjunctive*

Of the Imperfect Subjunctive the best explanation yet offered is perhaps that of Brugmann (*Grundr.* Ed. 2, II. Part 3, pp. 507 and 886) who regards it as a compound of the Present Infinitive with an old Imperfect Indicative of *eo* ' I go,' so that *regerēs* would be regarded as contracted from **regere ēi̯-es* ' you were going to rule, were to rule.' This would explain the Past sense of the forms very well ; but it must remain doubtful until some further evidence of the existence of such an Imperfect of *eo* in Latin is found.

INDICES

In both parts the numbers refer to the sections, unless they are preceded by p. *when they refer to pages.*

A. INDEX OF MATTERS

B. INDEX OF WORDS

I. LATIN

133

iuventa, 215

lacrima, 165
largiter, 270
lātē, 267
lātus, 158
laudābo, 285
laudant, 281
laudās, 281
laudo, 281
lautus, 115
lavācrum, 195
lēgī, 299
legimus, 122, 274
legitis, 274
legūmen, 170
levis, 246
līma, 248
lingua, 165
lino, 275
linquo, 282 (1)
loca, 210
locī, 210
longiter, 270
lōtus, 115
lūbricus, 193
lūceo, 191
lūcidus, 227, 238
lūmen, 249
lūna, 191, 249
lupa, 212
lupus, 169

magis, 252
magister, 252, 253
magistrātus, 230
maior, 140
Manios, p. 11
marcidus, 202
māter, 57, 250
māteria, 231
māteriēs, 231
Matuta, 118 (n)

maximus, 123, 255
maxomos, 255
maxumus, 123
medicīna, 214
medius, 177
melior, 252
melius, 272
mēns, 92
meretōd, 163
mīlitāris, 195
Minerva, 151
minister, 252
mīror, 193
miser, 188
missus, 166
mittere, 109 (2)
modō and *modo*, 15–16, 205
moenia, 117
mollis, 104 (2)
molta, 198
monēbam, 284
monēbo, 285
moneo, 106, 136, 281
monērī, 317
monimentum, 123
monitor, 79
monui, 302
monumentum, 123
mōtus, 144
muccus, 111
mūcus, 111
mulcāre, 198
mulierem, 94
multa, 198
multō, 266
multum, 268
mūnia, 117
mūnus, 117
muttus, 184

nauta, 215
navebos, 127
nāvis, 219

2. GREEK

3. FRENCH

4. ITALIAN

5. GERMAN

6. ENGLISH

THE END